T0311918

Kuala Lumpur

Kuala Lumpur is a diverse city representing many different religions and nationalities. Recent government policy has actively promoted unity and cohesion throughout the city; and the country of Malaysia, with the implementation of a programme called 1Malaysia. In this book, the authors investigate the aims of this programme—predominantly to unify the Malaysian society—and how these objectives resonate in the daily spatial practices of the city's residents.

This book argues that elements of urban infrastructure could work as an essential mediator 'beyond community', allowing inclusive social structures to be built, despite cultural and religious tensions existing within the city. It builds on the premise of an empirical study which explores the ways in which different communities use the same spaces, supported through the implementation of a theoretical framework which looks at both Western and Islamic conceptualisations of the notion of community. Through the analysis of Kuala Lumpur, this book contributes towards the creation of more inclusive places in multi-ethnic, multi-cultural and multi-religious communities across the world.

Marek Kozlowski is currently a Senior Lecturer and Master of Tropical Urban Design Program Coordinator at the Faculty of Design and Architecture, University Putra Malaysia. He has worked as an urban designer on several key projects in Australia, Malaysia, United Arab Emirates, Saudi Arabia, Oman and Poland. He has conducted visiting lectures at universities in Australia, Brunei, Malaysia, Indonesia, China, Thailand and Poland. He has written several publications in the field of urban design and planning including a book *Urban Design: Shaping the Attractiveness of the Urban Environment with the End-Users*.

Asma Mehan is the current Postdoctoral Research Associate at CITTA (research center for territory, transports and environment) at the University of Porto, Portugal. She is an editor at *Architectural Histories*, the open-access journal of the European Architectural History Network (EAHN), and active member of the Association of European Schools of Planning (AESOP).

Krzysztof Nawratek is a Senior Lecturer in Humanities and Architecture at the University of Sheffield, UK. He is an author of *City as a Political Idea* (2011), *Holes in the Whole. Introduction to urban revolutions* (2012), *Radical Inclusivity. Architecture and Urbanism* (ed. 2015), *Urban Re-Industrialisation* (ed. 2017) and *Total Urban Mobilisation. Ernst Junger and Postcapitalist City* (2018).

Built Environment City Studies

The *Built Environment City Studies* series provides researchers and academics with a detailed look at individual cities through a specific lens. These concise books delve into a case study of an international city, focusing on a key built environment topic. Written by scholars from around the world, the collection provides a library of thorough studies into trends, developments and approaches that affect our cities.

Baltimore
Reinventing an Industrial Legacy City
Klaus Philipsen

Milan
Productions, Spatial Patterns and Urban Change
Edited by Simonetta Armondi and Stefano Di Vita

Baghdad
An Urban History through the Lens of Literature
Iman Al-Attar

Istanbul
Informal Settlements and Generative Urbanism
Noah Billig

Rio de Janeiro
Urban Expansion and Environment
José L. S. Gámez, Zhongjie Lin and Jeffrey S. Nesbit

Kuala Lumpur
Community, Infrastructure and Urban Inclusivity
Marek Kozlowski, Asma Mehan and Krzysztof Nawratek

For more information about this series, please visit: www.routledge.com/

Kuala Lumpur

Community, Infrastructure and Urban Inclusivity

Marek Kozlowski, Asma Mehan and Krzysztof Nawratek

Routledge
Taylor & Francis Group

LONDON AND NEW YORK

First published 2020
by Routledge
4 Park Square, Milton Park, Abingdon, Oxon OX14 4RN

and by Routledge
605 Third Avenue, New York, NY 10017

First issued in paperback 2022

Routledge is an imprint of the Taylor & Francis Group, an informa business

Publisher's Note
The publisher has gone to great lengths to ensure the quality of this reprint but points out that some imperfections in the original copies may be apparent.

British Library Cataloguing-in-Publication Data
A catalogue record for this book is available from the British Library

Library of Congress Cataloging-in-Publication Data
Names: Kozlowski, Marek (Urban designer), author. |
Mehan, Asma, author. | Nawratek, Krzysztof, 1970- author.
Title: Kuala Lumpur: community, infrastructure and urban inclusivity / Marek Kozlowski, Asma Mehan and Krzysztof Nawratek.
Description: New York, NY: Routledge, 2020. | Series: Built environment city studies | Includes bibliographical references and index.
Identifiers: LCCN 2019047297 (print) | LCCN 2019047298 (ebook) | ISBN 9781138207387 (hardback) | ISBN 9781315462417 (ebook)
Subjects: LCSH: Sociology, Urban—Malaysia—Kuala Lumpur. | Urban ecology (Sociology)—Malaysia—Kuala Lumpur. | City planning—Malaysia—Kuala Lumpur. | Public spaces—Malaysia—Kuala Lumpur. | Kuala Lumpur (Malaysia)—Social conditions.
Classification: LCC HN700.6.K78 K69 2020 (print) | LCC HN700.6.K78 (ebook) | DDC 307.7609595/1—dc23
LC record available at https://lccn.loc.gov/2019047297
LC ebook record available at https://lccn.loc.gov/2019047298

ISBN 13: 978-1-03-247483-0 (pbk)
ISBN 13: 978-1-138-20738-7 (hbk)
ISBN 13: 978-1-315-46241-7 (ebk)

DOI: 10.4324/9781315462417

Typeset in Times New Roman
by codeMantra

Contents

Preface

Kuala Lumpur, the capital of Malaysia, is a unique city in terms of its sense of place and identity, history and development and strong ethnic diversity. When Malaysia's first Prime Minister proclaimed independence on 31.08.1957, Kuala Lumpur was a medium-size administrative city with a population of just over 360,000. It was significantly smaller than other Southeast Asia capitals, and even within the Malay Peninsula, it was overshadowed by Singapore and Penang.

Although this book refers to the city of Kuala Lumpur, it is almost impossible to discuss and evaluate Kuala Lumpur without looking at the entire surrounding urban conurbation. The existing boundaries of Kuala Lumpur were designated in 1974 when most of today's satellite cities either did not exist or were in their premature form of evolution. Today's boundaries of KL are administrative and do not follow any geographical urban edge or natural frontier. The main international gateway to KL via air is located in Sepang and by the sea in Port Klang. Both cities are located well outside the existing Kuala Lumpur official city boundaries.

Contemporary Kuala Lumpur is a major urban centre in Southeast Asia competing with other capitals of the region. The city administrative area under the jurisdiction of the local authority Kuala Lumpur Municipal Council (Dewan Bandaraya Kuala Lumpur) has a population of 1.7 million and covers the area of 243 km^2. The population of the Kuala Lumpur urban conurbation covering an area around 2,700 sq.km is 7.7 million (World Population Review, 2018). The most popular names given to the KL urban conurbation are the KL-Klang Region, Greater Kuala Lumpur or the Kuala Lumpur Metropolitan Region. In this book, we are using the name Kuala Lumpur Metropolitan Region (KLMR).

For this study, the city of Kuala Lumpur is identified as the core area of interest, analysis and evaluation while the Kuala Lumpur

Metropolitan Region is the surrounding context area. The surrounding context area is investigated in terms of its specific relations to the core area. The context area encompasses major urban centres, including the Kuala Lumpur International Airport in Sepang, the multimedia city Cyberjaya, Shah Alam, the capital of the state of Selangor and Putrajaya the new federal administrative capital of Malaysia.

The area of KLMR covers ten municipalities, including Kuala Lumpur, Putrajaya, Shah Alam, Petaling Jaya, Klang, Kajang, Subang Jaya, Selayang Ampang Jaya and Sepang (International Urban Development Association, 2015). The map of KLMR is shown in Figure 0.1

The urban structure of the metropolitan region is polycentric and based on a hierarchical distribution of centres connected by a network of transport corridors very similar arrangement to a typical model of an American post-industrial city. However, the city of Kuala Lumpur is still the prime globalised centre with the highest intensity of multinational companies, prominent landmarks and activity nodes. This makes Kuala Lumpur the primary centre of the urban conurbation.

Figure 0.1 Kuala Lumpur core area of investigation and the surrounding context area the Kuala Lumpur Metropolitan Region.

Source: F. Adnan and M. Kozlowski.

The principal centres include Shah Alam, Petaling Jaya and Subang Jaya, while there are several major centres such as Bangi, Serdang, Gombak or Rawang. The specialised centres include the Kuala Lumpur International Airport in Sepang and Cyberjaya the new multi-media city. Putrajaya, the new administrative capital of Malaysia, constitutes a principal institutional centre.

This book looks at three major elements of the urban environment: the urban community, the spatial urban growth and inclusivity, and the urban and social infrastructures. The community of Kuala Lumpur is examined in terms of their religious affiliations, social habits and multi-ethnic interrelations. Kuala Lumpur is a city where religion is a permanent feature of the urban landscape. There are hundreds of Mosques all located within the proximity of residential and employment areas. There is also a significant number of Hindu, Chinese temples and Christian churches. The Holy Month of Ramadan followed by Eid, Chinese New Year and Christmas always leave a visible mark on the city's urban landscape. The Hindu Festival of Thaipusam draws tens of thousands of pilgrims every year. Yet despite the strong religious and traditional influences, there is another side of Kuala Lumpur described in the book by Ewe Paik Leong 'Kuala Lumpur Undercover'. Paik Leong describes the sleazy precincts of the inner and central city areas characterised by night clubs and massage parlours. This 'Dr Jekyll and Mr Hyde' face of the city adds to the uniqueness and diversity of its urban environment.

Kuala Lumpur, which had its beginnings as a tin mining settlement, has been influenced in its trajectory of growth by various political and economic determinants. Throughout the 19th and half of the 20th century, the British had a significant influence on the development of the urban form and structure. The majority of urban planning policies and regulations derived directly from the British planning system. Even today's planning system in Malaysia is based on the British planning system. The Chinese being the predominant ethnic group determined the architectural pattern of the city by introducing the famous two-three storey shop-houses. After independence, the political agenda was to bring the Malay population to the city and its vicinity. This sparked the development of edge cities and new residential townships.

Since the 1990s globalisation, neoliberalism and property-led development took the leading role in shaping the growth and development of the Kuala Lumpur Metropolitan Region. As a result of global forces, the region has witnessed two major changes. First, the office and up-market housing development, producer services and international service sector have been located in the new Kuala Lumpur City

Centre (KLCC). Second, a semi-urban corridor called Multimedia Super Corridor (MSC) has emerged, including Kuala Lumpur Central City (KLCC), Putrajaya, Cyberjaya and the Kuala Lumpur International Airport (KLIA). In the 1990s, Malaysia's federal government commenced on the development of Putrajaya, located 25 km south of Kuala Lumpur within the new Multimedia Super Corridor that stretches a further 40 km south to the new Kuala Lumpur International Airport (Rimmer and Dick, 2009; Kozlowski, 2014).

The current dynamic growth of the KLMR is uncoordinated without any regional plan and any regional governance. This rapid development often neglects the local tropical climate, the sense of place and identity. It is also in total contrast with the old Confucian philosophy promoting a modest and humble growth of the urban environment (Lui, 2015).

Urban infrastructure in Kuala Lumpur and the rest of Malaysia has been traditionally managed and coordinated by the federal, state and local governments. That situation drastically changed in the 1990s when Malaysia witnessed a spree of privatisation including water supply, solid waste disposal, energy supply and telecommunications. This neoliberal trend also affected the social infrastructure including the health and education sectors. Today the KLMR has a high concentration of tertiary educational establishments outrunning the public educational institutions.

The book focuses mainly on the use of qualitative research methods. The major qualitative research methods include review of public documents, observations and structured interviews with major stakeholders involved in the planning and development of the Greater Kuala Lumpur Region.

Methods and techniques used in this study include primary and secondary data collection and structured interviews with representatives of government departments and NGOs.

The structure and arrangement of each chapter largely depend on the topic and type of investigation. However, every chapter has a short introduction and major findings.

Chapter 1 introduces the idea of radical inclusivity as a significant effort to create a universal ontological framework that supersedes religious, national, economic or ethnic divisions. This chapter analyses Malaysian conceptualisations of the notion of 'community', critically comparing its Western traditions, Anglo-Saxon colonial practices and legacy with the Islamic idea of the Ummah and Islamic approaches to non-Muslim communities. The purpose of this chapter is to define a theoretical context framing the investigation that follows.

Chapter 2 discusses the theoretical framework developed by Michel de Certeau and Henri Lefebvre within a context set out by Susan Leigh Star's notion of 'boundary object', in order to conceptualize the relationship between citizens of KL and the socio-spatial infrastructure of the city. This highly theoretical chapter suggests how and to what extent the strategic level of urban regulations, political frameworks and religious and cultural differences may be 'ignored' by residents of KL and will discuss possibility of focusing on material infrastructure as a medium through which cultural differences can be overcome (due to its unintended 'openness' and 'partial neutrality'). The chapter works as a theoretical foundation for more case-related following chapters.

Chapter 3 examines the current ethnic pattern in KLMR and discusses the legal framework behind the current ethnic divisions. It explores the mechanisms that created the platform allowing for the overwhelming Malay dominance in governance and administration. Its implications on the physical and social urban environment are portrayed by showing a few case study examples. The chapter also touches on the migrant communities of Kuala Lumpur. The second part of the chapter identifies different types of urban spaces and describes human activities taking place. This is followed by observations seeking to determine how different public spaces are used by different ethnic groups.

Chapter 4 traces the different steps of evolution of Kuala Lumpur from a tin mining settlement to a medium-size city after the Second World War, an emerging urban conurbation after independence, the rapidly expanding urban region during the Mahathir era and the current globalised megacity of today. It illustrates the drastic spatial change in the last 60 years from a tropical, friendly and inclusive city to a polarised and dynamic urban conurbation. To support the major findings and conclusions this chapter includes a structured interview and a questionnaire survey conducted on a sample of senior residents.

Chapter 5 describes the history and current state of the urban and social infrastructure of the KLMR. The urban infrastructure includes water supply, wastewater management, waste management, public transport, the road network, pedestrian and cycling network, energy supply and telecommunications. The second part of the chapter examines the social infrastructure such as hospitals and medical clinics, primary and secondary schools, tertiary educational institutions, cultural hubs, affordable housing and security, emergency and social welfare facilities. The culmination of the chapter is an in-depth analysis examining how neoliberal forces and trends triggered a comprehensive privatisation program targeting both urban and social infrastructures.

Chapter 6 attempts to theorise the main findings of the book. It discusses examples of socio-spatial infrastructure in KL used by citizens from different religious, ethnic and economic backgrounds. The chapter aims to illustrate the spatiality and materiality of the mechanism of inclusion and exclusion. Similarities and differences between how (and when) members of different communities are using the same spaces are explored. The role of material infrastructure as a mediator between different communities is examined. The chapter puts the findings of the book into the theoretical framework of ANT/STS, providing some references to New Materialism as a useful conceptual framework.

The book attempts to tell the story of Kuala Lumpur as a particular example of a non-Western global city, where diverse religious and cultural forces are shaping the urban environment. The approach in this book suggests that the terms and concepts used to describe Western cities are not necessarily and entirely useful while talking about a city like Kuala Lumpur. In this city particular climate, a strong presence of Islam and (at least) two other religions, colonial past, neoliberal globalism and an <u>attempt</u> to define Malaysian identity shape the city in a very particular way. We would argue that Kuala Lumpur is not like any other city. Therefore the book is not providing any universal template to analyse other cities (even geographically close—like Singapour or Jakarta). At the same time, the book opens new paths of intellectual inquires in a growing interest in a decolonised urban theory.

1 Towards radical inclusivity– community, Ummah and beyond

Introduction

As the subject of the book suggests the purpose of the analysis is to determine how different religious and ethnic communities utilise space/ urban infrastructure in Kuala Lumpur (KL). This chapter introduces the idea of radical inclusivity as a significant effort to create a universal ontological framework that supersedes religious, national, economic or ethnic divisions. The aim is to test the hypothesis that the city produces non-consensual social structures—a kind of 'community of a higher order' which is not defined by a collective identity, but rather through co-dependence and co-living. The Malaysian conceptualisations of the notion of 'community', critically comparing its Western traditions, Anglo-Saxon colonial practices and legacy with the Islamic idea of the Ummah and Islamic approaches to non-Muslim communities are all analysed. This book focuses on the theory of an intellectual tool used to conduct research and guide the outcome of the empirical study. The purpose of this chapter is to define a theoretical context framing the investigation that follows.

The first part of the chapter explains in detail the notion of radical inclusivity and the Ummah as the Islamic notion of social unity.

Radical inclusivity

Radical inclusivity assumes an infinity of the universe; it assumes progress and constant change—also a change of hierarchies. There is a horizon of the whole, but there is no process of unification. In the urban scale, the city is the best environment to test the notion of radical inclusivity, since its space is 'naturally' used by a diverse range of people. Moreover, as a spatial entity, the city allows different (even contradictory) activities to happen at the same time. This section aims to explore the theoretical frameworks of the idea of 'Radical Inclusivity' to put the main argument in urban debates.

Radical or Absolute inclusivity has its roots in the Christian and Islamic Universalism (or in fact in any religion claiming the existence of Absolute); however, to have roots, it does not mean that radical inclusivity is exclusive to any religion. Focusing on the idea of 'inclusion', Carl Schmitt believes that "the specific political distinction to which political actions and motives can be reduced is that between friend and enemy". In this sense, the central argument of Schmitt's 'Concept of the Political' posits its juxtaposition in the dichotomy of friend versus enemy (Schmitt, 2007, p. 26). Jane Jacobs argues that definitions of 'self' and 'other' are building blocks for hierarchies of spatial power (Jacobs, 2002, p. 4). Focusing on the politics of identity enacted in urban space, Jacobs finds them as 'the struggles that produce promiscuous geographies of dwelling in place in which the categories of Self and Other, here and there, past and present, constantly solicit one another' (Jacobs, 2002, p. 5). The notion of inclusion can be rendered in Jacques Rancière's works as the inside-out dichotomy. He uses the concept of 'le partage du sensible' to describe the act of dividing between legitimate and illegitimate persons and forms of activity (Rancière, 2010, p. 60). In this definition, the sensible is precisely what can be thought, said, felt or perceived/the perceptible, the visible, etc. Rancière defines the urban space as a form of visibility that can serve as interruptions of the given partition of the sensible.

However, this dichotomy of friend and enemy is neither derived nor linked to another antithesis; instead, this binary grouping is independent and only corresponds to these other antitheses. As Torgovnick emphasised, we make sense of our world 'in the act of defining the other' (Torgovnick, 1999, p. 11). Similarly, Morton clarified that "western philosophy has traditionally defined 'the other'" as an object of consciousness for the western subject. This reductive definition has effectively destroyed the singular alterity of the other" (Morton, 2003, p. 37).' Focusing on Schmitt's concept of the political, Strauss argues that "the political – the grouping of humanity into friends and enemies – owes it legitimation to the seriousness of the question of what is right" (Strauss, 2007, p. 118).

On the other hand, Chinese philosopher Tingyang Zhao rejects Schmitt perspective on politics based on the distinction between a friend and a foe as a "...the typical wrong in western political consciousness, or subconsciousness, in which political impulse divides and breaks up the world" (Zhao, 2006, p. 34). Zhao believes that the Chinese system based on families differs fundamentally from the Western system based on individuals. Chinese political thinking is often criticised for its neglect of the individual as well as individual rights, but this is a misunderstanding of the Chinese Philosophy and a poor understanding of political society (Zhao, 2006, p. 33). He questions the value of focusing on an individual while discussing politics:

> There is no Chinese denial of the value of the individual, but rather a denial of the individual to be a political foundation or starting point, because the political makes sense only when it deals with 'relations' rather than 'individuals', and the political is meant to speak for co-existence rather than a single existence.
>
> (Zhao, 2006, p. 33)

As Giddens clarified the modern western political theory is based on the system of nation/states (Giddens, 1985), while the Chinese most significant political unit is the framework of world/society. In the book by Krzysztof Nawratek titled *Total Urban Mobilisation* the author emphasised that Zhao's idea of All-under-Heaven as a political project allows us to see the cities (and also fragments of cities) as socio-spatial and temporal beings while reaching the ultimate horizon of the worldness (Nawratek, 2019, p. 88). Nawratek added, "the city exists because there is 'another dimension' (the commons, the public) putting private domains in a broader context and allowing them to interact" (Nawratek, 2019, p. 83).

Within the context of contemporary politics, there are different logics (or tendencies) to define radical inclusivity. Following Ernesto Laclau's definition, radical inclusion can be considered as the populist logic of inclusion that employs a liberal universalist conception of inclusivity in which "the 99 per cent" is a taken-for-granted category and understood to exist in itself (Laclau, 2005). Some other scholars believe that the radical politics of inclusion enacted through anti-oppressive practices in which ideals of inclusivity are understood as a process and a struggle. In the recent occupy movements, inclusivity is not just about the general participation in the movement, but also inherently tied to the procedures and practices through which decisions were made (Maharawal, 2013, p. 179). According to Gerald Raunig, radical inclusion means "to sustain and affirm the differences, and within them continue to differentiate, multiply, in a continuous expansion of multiplicity" (Raunig, 2014, p. 34). Moreover, radical inclusion involves the "reterritorialization of space and time", allowing for "a fundamentally inclusive territory without doors or thresholds, not surrounded or traversed from the outset by borders" (Raunig, 2014, p. 33). In this sense, radical inclusion recognises "a need for invention, innovation and multiplication of revolutionary practices and narratives" (Raunig, 2014, p. 34).

'Community' as a sociocultural paradigm

Robert Esposito, in his seminal book 'Communitas', defines a foundation of a community as an absence. He doesn't reject the communitarian understanding of its notion—as based on shared identity and values; but Esposito focuses his attention on a violent process of becoming a member of the community. The very act of birth violently puts a human being in specific social structures—family, nation, class. After that, every decision to join any community is grounded by a particular rite of passage—to become a part of a community one must change (or/and paid a specific price). Community imposes on us liabilities of obligations—even if belonging to the community is seen as a gift. Esposito writes about the 'gift' of Eucharist, through which Catholics become part of the church, defined as the mystical body of Christ—the same body that had been tortured and killed. What's more, this inclusion is something as alien as 'the body of God' tears us violently from our own individual identity. What Esposito ignores in his analysis is the fact that the Eucharist is a kind of mechanism/ infrastructure that exists outside members of the community allowing them to 'plug in' to the Absolute (Esposito, 2010).

The Islamic sociopolitical Philosopher—Abu Nasr Farabi— envisioned an ideal or perfect city, under a philosopher–king for humankind to attain happiness through living in an entirely guided city. Besides, Farabi believes that humans cannot reach the perfection they are destined to outside the framework of political societies. According to Farabi, this political understanding of the concept of the city has always entangled into the theological concepts (Mehan, 2016, p. 311).

Agamben in his book 'The Coming Community' emphasised that the coming community finds its place in a profound present and within the potentiality of change and transformation to open up a reflection on the idea of 'radical change' (Agamben, 1993, p. 222). For Agamben, the advanced capitalism produces a high accumulation of 'dispositivi' extending its paranoid forms of control with mechanisms of inclusion/exclusion, while politics has disappeared, supporting the governmental machine (Agamben, 1998). In Agamben's definitions, the term 'dispositivi' suggests a reflection on the sovereignty of life and governmentality (Agamben, 2009). In this interpretation, Jean Luc Nancy defined the community through the political nature of its resistance against immanent power (Nancy, 1991).

Similarly, Krzysztof Nawratek, in his book 'City as a political idea' created a notion of a-androgyne, who can interact with the world/other people because of its incompleteness (Nawratek, 2011). The problem with the community lies in its totality and unification—the community assumes a standard set of features that distinguish members of the community from those who are outside. But each of these features includes a (however small) mechanism of inclusion—this mechanism allows any community to expand, it also prevents the community against total unification. This 'inclusive remnants' (metaphorically could be defined as a 'free inclusive radicals') could be amplified to break through from the community itself and to become elements of 'inclusive infrastructure', not creating the community but building the commons. The infrastructure we can define as a semi-transcendent mechanism allowing diverse subjects to execute their agency.

Simone posits the concept of *People as infrastructure* as the residents' need to generate concrete acts and contexts of social collaboration inscribed with multiple identities rather than in overseeing and enforcing modulated transactions among discrete population groups (Simone, 2004, p. 419). Tingyang Zhao believes that the infrastructure connects subjects, allowing them to become 'political' by going beyond their individual existence; but infrastructure also allows subjects to redefine themselves, to strengthen its subjectivity. This dualistic way of operating of the infrastructure is possible only because the subject always exists and is defined in a context. It is always set in relation to other subjects. This relation is not necessarily equal or symmetrical, but nevertheless, it exists. The subject defines itself by an ability to look inside and to look outside. Therefore, the subject is a surface, it exists in-between (Zhao, 2006).

'Ummah': Islamic notion of social unity

Ummah (or Umma is an Arabic term literally means community or people) is often used in Quran, which had also shaped the historical consciousness of Muslims in early Islamic history, and it continues to affect the politics of Muslim states. Although the term Ummah is widely accepted by Muslims and Islamic scholars to refer to "community", "group" or "nation", it is used in 62 different forms in the Quran in relation to social, political and religious contexts (Denny, 1975, p. 43). Hasan argues that Ummah is constituted through a universal community, based on a shared faith, and the implementation of faith (Hasan, 2011, p. 145). In agreement, Bowen believes that Islamic culture promotes the sense of a worldwide community—Ummah—among ordinary Muslims (Bowen, 2006, p. 881).

As Abubakar pointed out, in the process of consolidation, the Muslim communities began to assume a distinct identity and to be organised based on three meeting principles: religion (Islam), territory (Hula) and nation (Bangsa). As a result, a new consciousness emerged amongst the Muslims as a people belonging not only to a local entity, but also as a part of the expanding world of Islam (literally Dar al-Islam, which is an Islamic term for the Muslim regions of the world) in Southeast Asia (Abubakar, 2010, p. 134).

Danny shows (in the particular passages) that the term Ummah (refers exclusively to the Muslims) are found in the Medinan period, that is the time after the Prophet Muhammad had migrated to the city of Medina (Denny, 1975, p. 45). He added "the concept of Ummah itself develops from a general one, applying to non-Arab groups, too, toward a more exclusive one which is limited to the Muslim community" (Denny, 1975, p. 36). It is also during the Medinan period that the concept of an 'um-matanwasatan' (justly balanced community) came into effect at a time when the Muslim religious community reached its most developed stage (Denny, 1975, pp. 54–55). In terms of Quranic exegesis, conceptions of al-wasatiyyah (which is derived from an Arabic word "wasat" and means middle, moderate, fair, just and setting) are generally associated with the perspectives, beliefs and actions of the individual, as well as notions of a collective community (Ummah) (Davids, 2017, p. 310).

While the Constitution of Medina (and the related concept of dār al-Islām) seems to sanction diversity within the Islamic communities, the concept of the Ummah refers to an ideal state, which is a repre-sentative of original all-encompassing unity. According to Arkoun, the concept of an ummatanwasatan (a justly balanced community) contains a theological inclusion of all people (Arkoun, 1994, p. 53). However, under the pressure of European colonial encroachment on Muslim domains and challenging the sociopolitical identity of Muslims, the Islamic resistance movement defends the Ummah to confront European powers (Dallal et al., n.d.).[1]

The western definition of the notion of Ummah within the context of political Islam may be termed by the French School of thought, which seemingly acknowledges the resilience of a transnational po-litical Islam, while stressed the deterritorialization of political Islam within Western Europe (Kepel, 2004; Roy, 2004). By comparing the no-tion of Ummah vis-à-vis the Western nation-state definition, it can be concluded that Muslims have gradually realised that the nation-state system has become an impediment in accomplishing their way of life and in bringing about the kind of ummatic cooperation and security they seek (Akram, 2007, p. 381). In this regard, the concept of Ummah stands for a certain kind of transnational unity which aims to define a social and political unit.

Islam in Malaysia

KL did not evolve as an Islamic city but as a rough 'cowboy style' tin mining settlement full of gambling dens, bars and brothels. Sprouting from a tin mining settlement it was built mainly by Chinese and other Asian migrant workers. On the eve of independence, in the late 1950s, the city was still predominantly Chinese; however, since the 1960s, through Federal Government policies and interventions, this status drastically changed. Today, the demographics in KL indicate that Malay/Bumiputera constitute 45.9%, the Chinese 43.2%, Indians 10.3% and others 1.6%. The percentage of the Malay population in satellite cities of the Kuala Lumpur Metropolitan Region (KLMR) built after independence is considerably higher. For example, the Malay population of Shah Alam is 65%, and in the new administrative capital of Putrajaya, Malays constitute an overwhelming 97% of the total population (World Population Review, 2018).

Pre-Islamic society in Malaysia was either mostly Hindu (in Malaya, or West Malaysia) or animistic (in Sabah and Sarawak,[2] or East Malaysia); and the law was, in general, based on custom (*adat*) (Harding, 2012b, p. 358). Starting from the 13th to 15th century, it is more than 500 years that Islam has fully embedded in Malay Society.[3] The 'embeddedness' of Malaysian Islam had been integrated within the Dutch and British colonial systems as well as Indian, Chinese and European major civilisations (that existed before and after Islam came to the shores of the Malay world (Aziz and Shamsul, 2004, p. 341). It is important to note that some scholars pointed out that the term 'Malay' was employed more broadly by European observers after the 16th century, which reflects the way people identified themselves in those centuries (Reid, 2001; Sutherland, 2001).

As the result of the fusion of at least three significant civilisations and two colonial systems, Peletz (2002) emphasised the importance of understanding the depth and breadth of the 'embeddedness' of Malaysian Islam within the many civilisations and colonialisms that existed before and after Islam came to the shores of the Malay world (Peletz, 2002). In the Malay States, Islamic law seems to have played an essential role as the personal and religious law of Muslims (mainly family law, succession, the law relating to mosques, and religious observance) while Malay Adat (customary law) played an essential role in criminal law and property, but only marginally in family law (Harding, 2012, p. 359).[4]

In the whole of South East Asia, Muslims make up 40% of the region's total population. In order of distribution, Indonesia has the largest Muslim majority of 88%, followed by Brunei with 67%, and Malaysia with 60% (Fealy and Hooker, 2006, p. 7; Saravanamuttu, 2010, p. 1). Utilising Islam as an ideological platform for nationalist movement is common throughout the Muslim world, including by Malay-Muslims in Malaysia (Milner, 1988). Anthony Burgess in his book Malay Trilogy written in the mid-1950s, just prior to Malaysia gaining its full independence, portrays Victor Crabbe, a British history teacher at an elite school for all the peninsula's ethnic groups—Malay, Chinese and Indian in a fictional town called Kuala Hantu (the school is modelled on the Malay College at Kuala Kangsar, Perak and Raffles Institution, Singapore). Burgess displays a society, where disregard of the ethnic group or religion, people socialise together even in clubs and bars. Such free social interaction would be a sporadic phenomenon in contemporary Malaysia where the ethnicity and religion have become a major determinant of one's social habits, social interaction and the way of life.

Reviewing the images of KL from the 1950s and 1960s, the perception is of a unified urban community disregard of race and religion. This is best manifested in the dressing styles applied by Chinese, Malay and Indian women who all followed the universal trends. Although the Malay ladies wore baju kurung and selendang, Indian ladies used sari during festivities and religious events[5] (Ahmad, 2017). A similar image of Malaysia was displayed after independence in the early 1960s in the movies directed by the most prominent icon of Malay entertainment P. Ramlee. In P. Ramlee movies, one could see Malays engaging in activities such as dancing or even alcohol drinking with a majority of women following western fashion trends. In contemporary Malaysian movies, the Malay community is shown in much different, non-western and traditional appearance.

In the 1970s, Malaysia experienced the unpredicted rise of a powerful and traditional Islamic movement that followed the implementation of programs designed to address 'Malay' economic disadvantage (Milner, 2008, p. 15). As a result of the Islamic revival movement that commenced in the late 1970s, this unified urban social environment gradually started to change. The conversion was evident in the dressing codes applied by Malay women who began to wear the head cover, commonly known as hijab. This was followed by the introduction of headscarves as part of a compulsory uniform for all Muslim school girls and the emergence of various hijab styles in magazines and the local mass media. Although wearing hijab is not mandatory, a majority of Malay women in Malaysia including the KLMR opt for using it on an everyday basis. The Islamic revival movement, which began in the 1970s, has given the Malay population a new sense of pride and identity (Ahmad, 2017).

Indeed, there is a clear relationship between ethnicity and religion: indeed, the definition of 'Malay' in the Constitution includes being Muslim.[6] However, not all Muslims are Malay; they include Indian Muslims and Chinese, Indian and Sabah/Sarawak native converts (Harding, 2012, p. 356). In Malaysia, a 'Malay' is said to be someone who (in addition to fulfilling specific residential requirements) "professes the Muslim religion, habitually speaks the Malay language, (and) conforms to Malay custom (adat)" [7] (Siddique, 1981, p. 77). Milner believes that expressions such as 'Malay proper', 'authentic Malay culture', 'authentic Malays', 'ordinary Malays' and 'pure Malay' are also often used in the accounts of researchers in a way that can seem to allude to some core or typical 'Malay' community (Milner, 2008, p. 7). Milner added that specific forces operated to promote unity, especially when 'Malays' confront outsiders. He uses the example of the Malays' of Singapore in the immediate post World War II period, which was said to feel "considerable in-group solidarity" as one "discrete section" of the island's multi-ethnic assemblage (Djamour, 1959, p. 22; Milner, 2008, p. 8). However, in recent years, religion has, to some extent, replaced ethnicity in defining identity and interest in what has become a complex and contested polity (Harding, 2012; Nawratek and Mehan, 2018).

In the Malay world, the ulama (religious specialist), who were trained in traditional Islamic education, confronted and resisted the encroachment of western imperialism, articulated in the form of the anti-colonial movement (Aziz and Shamsul, 2004, p. 349).

The Malaysian Constitution became the single most important modern institutional tool that moulded and conditioned Malaysian Islam, thus defining its sociopolitical space in Malaysian government and politics (Aziz and Shamsul, 2004, p. 351). The Malaysian religion can be considered as a state matter that is under the supervision of the Federal Constitution. However, the Islamisation process in Malaysia with a large minority population (approximately 35%) of non-Muslims has moved faster over the last 40 years (Olivier, 2016, p. 267). The Islamic policies of successive administrations from that of Tunku Abdul Rahman (a Malaysian politician who became Malaya's first Prime Minister after independence in 1957) to Mahathir Bin Mohamad (the current prime minister of Malaysia for the second time) have helped to elevate Islam's public profile to new heights. Moreover, the modernisation that the British had left was later accelerated under the premiership of Dr Mahathir Mohamad, who introduced the principles of political Islam in Malaysian society (Liow, 2004, p. 200).

The Malaysian government aims to direct the kind of Islam that must evolve in a modernising society like Malaysia. Concerning the government's definition of Islamic values, the federal government continues its Islamisation efforts by initiating the setting up of Islamic institutions of various kinds (Shamsul, 1997). Islamic law is effective in its scope to family law, and Muslim religious offences; hence, the Syariah (the Malay spelling of Sharia) courts have particular jurisdiction (Peletz, 2002). It is also to be noted that various *negeri* legislations in Malaysia, deal with the administration of Muslim laws. Furthermore, because the administration of Islamic matters and Malay customs is not centralised at the Federal level but under the jurisdiction of each negeri (state) religious bureaucracy and its ruler, the interpretation of some parts of the Syariah laws differs from negeri to negeri (Ibrahim, 1978).[8]

For this purpose, there are the institutions of the Islamic "mufti" (an Islamic scholar who interprets the Islamic law), Sharia courts, as well as the Islamic Religious Council in each state.

> The Islamic Religious Council was established through the provision of the state constitution as the central authority of the state on Islamic affairs second only to the state's royal patron. As long as the actions of the said Council are not in conflict with the Constitution, the state shall recognise the Council as a strategic institution that enhances the acquisition of knowledge (fardukifayah) of the Muslim community which also functions as the crucial last bastion in the ensuring of the continuity and survival of Islam and the Islamic community and society notwithstanding the prevalent political scenario in the country.
>
> (Hamid et al., 2015)

Today's KL portrays an image of a urban community with two major components: the traditional Muslims mainly comprising Malays and the contemporary groups whose members follow the globalised fashions, trends and patterns. The latter comprises mostly Chinese Malaysians, Indian Malaysians of non-Muslim faith and foreign tourists and expats. The two components coexist peacefully with each other but do not constitute a fully integrated society. The two communities have different dressing codes and lifestyles, however, can be spotted next to each other in many parts of the city, including public spaces, shopping, business and entertainment centres. An image of unified KL in the 1960s and a contemporary urban community is shown in a collage of images in Figure 1.1a–c.

Figure 1.1 (a and b, upper and centre) Women of Kuala Lumpur in the 1960s representing a unified community disregard race and religion. (c, lower) The urban community of contemporary Kuala Lumpur (below).

Sources: www.pinterest.com/pin/515662226072837205/ and M. Kozlowski and S. Szewczykowski.

Note: Upper and centre image is over 50 years old; therefore, it constitutes public property.

For the last 10 years, the Federal Government has made several attempts to better integrate the Malaysian community. The former Prime Minister Datuk Seri NajibTun Abdul Razak launched the 1Malaysia concept as a platform to build upon the unique strength of the diversity of multiracial Malaysia (The Star Malaysia, 2010). The new Pakatan Harapan[9] government under Prime Minister Dr Tun Mahathir went one step forward and distributed several key ministries to Chinese Malaysian politician from the Chinese dominated DAP coalition party.[10] However, one of the pledges of the Pakatan Harapan when they were still in opposition was to ratify the International Convention on the Elimination of all Forms of Racism and Discrimination (ICERD) once elected. It should be noted that ICERD has been ratified by a majority of Muslim countries around the world. The attempt to confirm ICERD in 2018 resulted in massive demonstrations by the Malay population on the streets of KL and other major cities in Malaysia. The Malays were concerned that ICERD could end the privileges they enjoyed since the 1970s. As a result of community pressure, the government decided to withdraw from their election promise, and Malaysia still remains as one of the few countries in the world that have not ratified ICERD. The 'ICERD incident' implies that the differences along ethnic lines in contemporary KL and other major cities in Malaysia are likely to remain.

Major findings

KL, capital of Malaysia, is a city in which representatives of different religions and nationalities live together. The government is actively promoting national unity and cohesion through a program called '1Malaysia'. It is essential to investigate here how the ambition of this program— to unify Malaysian society—resonates in the daily spatial practices of the residents of KL. It is important to note that speaking at a press conference on 14th May of 2018, the current Prime Minister Dr Mahathir Mohamad, revealed that the 1Malaysia slogan and greeting will soon be a thing of the past. He added, "We may have to change to a different slogan, but we did not decide on a suitable slogan".

Although Malaysia is not labelled as a stronghold of religious extremism, the Malay community is very traditional, and a majority of them strictly follow the five pillars of Islam. According to the Pew Research Centre opinion poll survey published by the Los Angeles Times in 2016, around 52% of the population of Malaysia supports the introduction of strict Sharia law. This figure is significantly higher than in predominantly Muslim countries such as Indonesia and Turkey, where the percentage of the population supporting Sharia is 22% and 13%, respectively. Considering that 64% of the population in Malaysia is Muslim, this opinion poll implies that a majority of the Muslim population in Malaysia support Sharia law (Simmons, 2016). However, this figure is based on a sample of 1000 face-to-face interviews; therefore, the margin of error is too high for the value to be fully reliable. Nevertheless, even with a high margin of error, one can assume that traditionalism and conservatism are well embedded within the Malay community.

Focusing on the idea of community from the Islamic tradition, the idea of 'Ummah' is often understood as the community/society followers of Allah. In the history of Islamic thought, meaning of Ummah sometimes goes beyond the religious boundaries, relating to people sharing the same territory (as residents—both Muslims and Jews—of Medina) or even refers to the humanity as a whole. On several occasions, the notion of Ummah is associated with specific duties and obligations, which makes it close to the community defined by Esposito. Because the meaning of Ummah stretched between universalist and sectarian condition, we should not try to pin down any specific definition, but rather focus on a critical power of its 'discursive displacement'.

By considering the city as the entity that produces non-consensual social structures—a kind of 'community of a higher order' which is not defined by a collective identity, but preferably through codependence and coliving, this part represented the notion of community as a sociocultural paradigm based on the Western philosophy. This chapter tries to produce a basis to compare the western traditions with the notion of Ummah and Islamic approaches to non-Muslim communities.

Notes

1 Malaya (former name of today's Malaysia) was never a real British colony. Each Malay state had a British resident, and the British had a profound influence on the economy and policies; however, the executive, legislative and judicial powers lay with the State Sultans and Malay Civil Institutions. The South Asian countries (India, Pakistan, Bangladesh, Bhutan, Sri Lanka, Sikkim and Nepal) had British rule much earlier than Malaysia.
2 Sabah and Sarawak were initially parts of the Brunei sultan-ate, which was also culturally related to the states of Malaya. Hence, Islam was invariably the State religion, and the ruler was also the Head of Islam. In Penang, Malacca, Sabah and Sarawak, however, Islam is not the state religion, and the *Yang di- Pertuan Agong* (King at the federal level) serves as the Head of Islam. See Andrew Harding, 2012. Constitutionalism, Islam and National Identity in Malaysia. In: R. Grote & T. Rode, eds. *Constitutionalism in Islamic Countries: Between Upheaval and Continuity.* Oxford: Oxford University Press.

3 Islam came to Malaysia in the 14th century through Arab merchants and Sufi missionaries. For reading the detailed history of 'Arrival of Islam in the Malay world', see: Azmi Aziz & A. B. Shamsul (2004) The religious, the plural, the secular and the modern: a brief critical survey on Islam in Malaysia, *Inter-Asia Cultural Studies*, 5:3, 341–35.
4 These laws are different from other parts of the Muslim world, especially the Middle East.
5 Selendang is a thin transparent rectangular shape wrapped around the head and worn by Malay women during special occasions (Ahmad 2017). Baju kurung is a regional cloth worn by Malay women. Baju is a kind of frock coat, whose sleeve length is to the wrist; kurung is a kind of skirt, which is of the ankle length (UK essays).
6 Constitution of Malaysia, art. 160, sec. 2.
7 Although the phrase 'Malay Custom (adat)' is often mentioned, even between villages located in one region, there are different customs.
8 At the negeri level, both pondok and madrasah began to lose their influence in many parts of the country, particularly in the Malay-Muslim dominated negeri of Kelantan, Terengganu, Kedah and Perlis, in the 1950s and 1960s.
9 Pakatan Harapan is a new coalition in Malaysia opposed to the former long-term ruling Barisan National (BN) coalition. It comprises the Democratic Action Party (DAP), People's Justice Party, National Trust Party and Malaysian United Indigenous Party (www.pakatanharapan.com.my).
10 DAP, The Democratic Action Party. One of the coalition partners of the Pakatan Harapan Government that took office in May 2018. It is a social democratic party established in 1966. Its members derive mainly from the Chinese Malaysian community. www.dapmalaysia.org.

Bibliography

Abubakar, C. A. (2010) A Never-Ending War and the Struggle for Peace in the Southern Philippines. In: J. Saravanamuttu, ed. *Islam and Politics in Southeast Asia*. London and New York: Routledge Malaysian Studies Series, pp. 127–143.

Agamben, G. (1993) *The Coming Community*. Minneapolis: University of Minnesota Press.

Agamben, G. (1998) *HOMO SACER: Sovereign Power and Bare Life*. D. Heller-Roazen, trans. and ed. Stanford, CA: Stanford University Press.

Agamben, G. (2009) *What Is an Apparatus? And Other Essays*. Stanford, CA: Stanford University Press.

Ahmad M. H. (2017) The Popularisation of Hijab in Malaysia: Fashion versus Modesty. In: Y. Seng-Guan, ed. *Malaysian and Their Identities*. Petaling Jaya: Strategic Information and Research Centre, pp. 47–63.

Akram, E. (2007) Muslim Ummah and Its Link with Transnational Muslim Politics. *Islamic Studies*, 46(3), 381–415.

Arkoun, M. (1994) *Rethinking Islam: Common Questions, Uncommon Answers*. San Francisco, CA: Westview Press.

Aziz, A., and Shamsul, A. (2004) The Religious, the Plural, the Secular and the Modern: A Brief Critical Survey on Islam in Malaysia. *Inter-Asia Cultural Studies*, 5(3), 341–356.

Bowen, J. R. (2006) Beyond Migration: Islam as a Transnational Public Space. *Journal of Ethnic and Migration Studies*, 30(5), 879–894.

Dallal, A. S., Yoginder, S., and Moten, A. R. (n.d.) *Ummah.* www.oxfordislamicstudies.com/article/opr/t236/e0818.

Davids, N. (2017) Islam, Moderation, Radicalism, and Justly Balanced Communities. *Journal of Muslim Minority Affairs*, 37(3), 309–320.

Denny, F. (1975) The Meaning of 'Ummah' in the Qur'ān. *History of Religions*, 15(1), 34–70.

Djamour, J. (1959) *Malay Kinship and Marriage in Singapore.* London: Athlone Press.

Esposito, R. (2010) *Communitas: The Origin and Destiny of Community.* Stanford, CA: Stanford University Press.

Fealy, G., and Hooker, V. (2006) *Voices of Islam in Southeast Asia: A Contemporary Sourcebook.* Singapore: Institute of Southeast Asian Studies.

Giddens, A. (1985) *The Nation-State and Violence.* Cambridge: Polity Press.

Hamid, N. et al. (2015) Empowerment of the Muslim Community Development in the State of Selangor: The Role of the Selangor State Islamic Religious Council. *The e-Journal of Sultan AlauddinSulaiman Shah*, 2(1), 1–12

Harding, A. (2012a) Constitutionalism, Islam, and National Identity in Malaysia. In: R. Grote and T. Rode, eds. *Constitutionalism in Islamic Countries: Between Upheaval and Continuity.* Oxford: Oxford University Press, pp. 201–217

Harding, A. (2012b) Malaysia: Religious Pluralism and the Constitution in a Contested Polity. *Middle East Law and Governance*, 4, 356–385.

Hasan, M. (2011) The Concept of Globalization and How This Impacted on Contemporary Muslim Understanding of Ummah. *Journal of Globalization Studies*, 2(2), 145–159.

Ibrahim, A. (1978) The Position of Islam in the Constitution. In: T. M. Suffian, H. P. Lee and F. A. Trindade, eds. *The Constitution of Malaysia, It Development: 1957–1977, Kuala Lumpur.* Oxford: Oxford University Press, pp. 41–68.

Jacobs, J. (2002) *Edge of Empire: Postcolonialism and the City.* New York: Routledge.

Kepel, G. (2004) *The War for Muslim Minds: Islam and the West.* Cambridge, MA: Belknap of Harvard University Press.

Laclau, E. (2005) *On Populist Reason.* New York: Verso.

Liow, J. C. (2004) Political Islam in Malaysia: Problematising Discourse and Practice in the UMNO–PAS 'Islamisation Race'. *Commonwealth & Comparative Politics*, 42(2), 184–205.

Maharawal, M. (2013) Occupy Wall Street and a Radical Politics of Inclusion. *Sociological Quarterly*, 54(2), 177–181.

Mehan, A. (2016) Blank Slate: Squares and Political Order If the City. *Journal of Architecture and Urbanism*, 40(4), 311–321.

Milner, A. (1988) Islam and the Muslim State. In: M. B. Hooker, ed. *Islam in Southeast Asia*. Leiden: Brill, pp. 23–49.

Milner, A. (2008) *The Malays*. Chichester: Wiley-Blackwell.

Morton, S. (2003) *GayatriChakravortySpivak*. London: Routledge.

Nancy, J. L. (1991) *The Inoperative Community*. Minneapolis and Oxford: University of Minnesota Press.

Nawratek, K. (2011) *City as a Political Idea*. Plymouth: University of Plymouth Press.

Nawratek, K. (2019) Assemblages, Series, and Empire. In: K. Nawratek, ed. *Total Urban Mobilisation: Ernst Jünger and the Post-Capitalist City*. Singapore: Palgrave Pivot, pp. 79–89.

Nawratek, K., and Mehan, A. (2018) Producing Public Space Under the Gaze of Allah: Hetrosexual Muslims Dating in Kuala Lumpur. RGS-IBG Annual International Conference 2018, Cardiff University, UK.

Olivier, B. (2016) The Malaysian Islamization Phenomenon: The Underlying Dynamics and Their Impact on Muslim Women. *Islam and Christian–Muslim Relations*, 27(3), 267–282.

Peletz, M. (2002) *Islamic Modern: Religious Courts and Cultural Politics in Malaysia*. Princeton, NJ: Princeton University Press.

Ranciere, J. (2010) *Dissensus: On Politics and Aesthetics*. S. Corcoran, trans. and ed. London: Continuum.

Raunig, G. (2014, n-1) Making Multiplicity: A Philosophical Manifesto. In: N. Papastergiadis and V. Lynn, eds. *Art in the Global Present*. Sydney: UTSe Press, pp. 31–44.

Reid, A. (2001) Understanding Melayu (Malay) as a Source of Diverse Modern Identities. *Journal of Southeast Asian Studies*, 32(3), 295–313.

Roy, O. (2004) *Globalised Islam: The Search for a New Ummah*. New York: Columbia University Press.

Saravanamuttu, J. (2010) Majority–Minority Muslim Politics and Democracy. In: J. Saravanamuttu, ed. *Islam and Politics in Southeast Asia*. London and New York: Routledge, pp. 1–17.

Schmitt, C. (2007) *The Concept of the Political*. Chicago, IL: University of Chicago Press.

Shamsul, A. (1997) Identity Construction, Nation Formation, and Islamic Revivalism in Malaysia. In: R. W. Hefner and P. Horvatich, eds. *Islam in an Era of Nation-States: Politics and Religious Renewal in Muslim Southeast Asia*. Honolulu: University of Hawai'i Press, pp. 207–227.

Siddique, S. (1981) Some Aspects of Malay-Muslim Ethnicity in Peninsular Malaysia. *Contemporary Southeast Asia*, 3(1), 76–87.

Simmons, A. M. (2016) Muslim World Sharply Divided on Koran's Influence on Government Law, Poll Finds. *Los Angeles Times*, 28 April.

Simone, A. (2004) People as Infrastructure: Intersecting Fragments in Johannesburg. *Public Culture*, 16(3), 407–429.

Strauss, L. (2007) Notes on Carl Schmitt. In: T. J. Lomax, trans. and ed. *The Concept of the Political.* Chicago, IL: University of Chicago Press, pp. 97–122.

Sutherland, H. (2001) The Makassar Malays: Adaptation and Identity, c. 1660–1790. *Journal of Southeast Asian Studies,* 32(3), 397–421.

Torgovnick, M. (1999) *Gone Primitive: Savage Intellects, Modern Lives.* Chicago, IL: University of Chicago Press.

The Star Malaysia (2010) Understanding 1Malaysia. www.thestar.com.my/news/nation/2010/12/15/understanding-1malaysia/

UK Essays (2019) History of BajuKurong. www.ukessays.com/essays/fashion/malay-woman-and-the-baju-kurung.php

World Population Review (2018) Kuala Lumpur Population 2018. http://worldpopulationreview.com/world-cities/kuala-lumpur-population/

Zhao, T. (2006) Rethinking Empire from a Chinese Concept 'All-under-Heaven' (Tian-xia). *Social Identities,* 12(1), 29–41.

2　From strategy to tactic

Introduction

This chapter discusses the theoretical framework developed by Michel de Certeau and Henri Lefebvre within a context set out by Susan Leigh Star's notion of 'boundary object', to conceptualise the relationship between citizens of Kuala Lumpur (KL) and the socio-spatial infrastructure of the city. This highly theoretical chapter suggests how and to what extent the strategic level of urban regulations, political frameworks and religious and cultural differences may be 'ignored' by residents of KL. This chapter will also discuss the possibility of focusing on material infrastructure as a medium through which cultural differences can be overcome (due to its unintended 'openness' and 'partial neutrality'). This chapter works as a theoretical foundation for following case study chapters.

'Strategies' and 'Tactics'

> To the ordinary man, to a common hero, a ubiquitous character, walking in countless thousands on the streets. In invoking here at the outset of my narratives the absent figure who provides both their beginning and their necessity, I inquire into the desire whose impossible object he represents. What are we asking this oracle whose voice is almost indistinguishable from the rumble of history to license us, to authorize us to say, when we dedicate to him the writing that one formerly offered in praise of the gods or the inspiring muses?
>
> (Certeau, 1984, p. V)

This part focuses on Michel de Certeau's concepts of strategies and tactics. It tries to distinguish between the two terms in forms and its apparatuses in daily life practices. The notion of tactics operating at the intersections of strategic constraints is a recruiting theme in Michel de Certeau's work (Certeau, 1984). Certeau, in his book "The Practice of Everyday Life", emphasised the significance of ordinary people's practices and action schemes as the multiple domains that display societal data. Certeau believes that power relations are enacted through an unfolding performance between 'strategies' and 'tactics'. In his terms, 'strategies' refers to those people, institutions and things that draw boundaries around the place and declare ownership. On the other hand, 'tactics' are the practices of the marginal that use timing to usurp the spatial limits imposed by the powerful (Certeau, 1984). In this interpretation, 'strategies' have their boundaries and borders, because their existence depends upon the hegemonic structure that they located in it.

As Michel de Certeau explains:

> I call a "strategy" the calculus of force-relationships which becomes possible when a subject of will and power (a proprietor, an enterprise, a city, a scientific institution) can be isolated from an "environment." A strategy assumes a place that can be circumscribed as proper (and thus serve as the basis for generating relations with an exterior distinct from it (competitors, adversaries, "clienteles," "targets," or "objects" of research). Political, economic, and scientific rationality has been constructed on this strategic model.
>
> (Certeau, 1984, p. 17)

On the other hand, a tactic depends upon the utilisation of time and is rather 'inside holes and gaps strategy creates' that lacks permanent position. When circumstances require, tactics develop the crucial practices that are interferences to power mechanisms. About the relationship between 'tactics' and the dimension of time, Certeau points out:

> because it does not have a place, a tactic depends on time-it is always on the watch for opportunities that must be seized "on the wing." Whatever it wins, it does not keep. It must always manipulate events to turn them into opportunities." The weak must continually turn to their own ends forces alien to them. This is achieved in the propitious moments when they are able to combine heterogeneous elements (thus, in the supermarket, the housewife confronts heterogeneous and mobile data what she has in the refrigerator, the tastes, appetites, and moods of her guests, the best buys and their possible combinations with what she already has

on hand at home, etc.); the intellectual synthesis of these given elements takes the form, however, not of a discourse, but of the decision itself, the act and manner in which the opportunity is "seized."

(Certeau, 1984, p. 17)

Certeau's 'Strategies and Tactics' theory offers an organizing model to understand society and to produce a place. For Certeau, a tactic is a calculation determined by the absence of a proper locus. In his words, "the space of the tactic is the space of the other" (Certeau, 1984, pp. 36–37).

Certeau finds a way of grasping the 'timing' of the different cultural activities that are rendered both 'inert' and 'timeless'. For more or less the same reason, Certeau avoids to extract the documents from their historical context and aims to operate the speakers in particular situations of time, place and competition (Certeau, 1984, p. 20).

Buchanan believes that the essential difference between the two is the way they relate to the variables that everyday life inevitably throws at us all. He further added that "strategy is a technique of place, and tactics is a technique of space" (Buchanan, 2000, p. 89). For emphasizing the role of 'ordinary', Michel de Certeau's popular conceptualisation as 'strategies' and 'tactics' has also been interpreted as the power of powerless, the activism of the passive and the production of non-producers (Buchanan, 2000).

François Jullien—French Sinologist—in his book—The Propensity of Things—uses the Chinese concept of shi, meaning disposition of circumstance, power or potential to uncover the Chinese mode of thinking. Jullien begins with a single Chinese term, shi and follows its appearance from military strategy to politics and from reflection on history to "first philosophy" (Jullien, 1995). In Chinese philosophy, the relationship between tactics and strategy is akin to that of the logic of the reversal of shi (Buchanan, 2000, p. 102). As Jullien points out: "On the one hand, every tendency, once born, is naturally inclined to grow; on the other hand, any tendency carried to its ultimate limit becomes exhausted and cries out for reversal" (Jullien, 1995, p. 194). On this view, tactics have a propensity to become strategy, so the little victories of everyday life have the potential to disrupt the fatality of the established order.

Following the Buchanan diagram, in this chapter, the strategy will translate to infrastructure and tactic as the interaction with infrastructure. The related example is coming from Chapter 5 which discusses the urban infrastructure in Kuala Lumpur Metropolitan Region (KLMR). In this interpretation, time is an important parameter as the certain rhythm of the city allows different individuals and

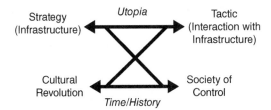

Figure 2.1 The relationship between tactics and strategy. Redrawn by the authors based on Buchanan's diagram. See Ian Buchanan, *Michel de Certeau: Cultural Theorist* (London: SAGE Publications, 2000), 105.

groups to use the same space and infrastructure. So, segregation and interactions are space and time-related. Since the 1990s, Malaysia followed the main principles of neo-liberalism and gradually privatised the necessary urban services, where the main actions in "tactics and strategies" emerged from the confrontation between the users of the city and urban planners and decision-makers. In this interpretation, the requalification of urban infrastructure in KL can be translated as a "Strategy" of the government in association with the private power to improve the public quality of life. The discussion in other chapters of this book indicates that in Malaysia there is a gap between what is "decided" and what happens (Figure 2.1).

Asian urbanism and materialities of infrastructure

As urban studies have taken a "southern turn", with an increasing number of works on the cities of global south, the rising contrast between built form and living spaces is critical. Seth Schindler argues that cities in the global South are fundamentally different from their Northern counterparts in a number of ways, and he offers three tendencies of urbanity that characterise many Southern cities—albeit in varying combinations and manifestations—and inform a paradigm of Southern urbanism. As the first important factor, Schindler believes that many cities in the global South have accumulated more capital and labour than at any time in their respective histories, yet they remain intractably disconnected. As the second tendency, Schindler argues that the metabolic configurations of the southern cities are discontinuous, dynamic and contested. Finally, he argues that the materiality and political economy are always already co-constituted in Southern Cities, so neither can be reduced to structure or context (Schindler, 2017).

According to Bunnell, "Asian cities are increasingly imagined as global frontiers of urban studies in the twenty-first century" (Bunnell, 2017, p. 9). In Southeast Asia, urbanization and rapid population growth are two significant, inevitable consequences of economic development (Ooi, 2005). In Asia, the urban become "an important site in which national developmental politics render itself visible, in which the national state attempts to render populations legible and governable", as well as being "a site where ruling powers try to legitimise their power but also accommodate some of the criticisms against it" (Doucette and Park, 2018, p. 401). Here, it is important to note for avoiding the trap of "Asian exceptionalism", we will follow the comparative urbanism viewpoint, which is in line with the perspective of Doreen Massey, who leads us to critically thinking of "a multiplicity of narratives" across Asia (Massey, 1999, p. 281).

In recent decades, scholars have analysed how infrastructures mediate exchange over distance, bringing different people, objects and spaces into interaction and forming the base on which to operate modern economic and social systems (Lefebvre, 1991; Graham and Marvin, 2001). In a general definition, infrastructures are the structural elements that allow goods and services to move between different people and places (Hardwicke, 2008).[1] Availability of and access to urban infrastructures support the daily requirements of the urban population, which resulted in the health of urban areas. The urban infrastructures' provision determines how the city regions can sustain their ever-growing population (Choguill, 1996). The availability of urban infrastructure helps cities maintain their competitive edge in the highly competitive global environment (Corey, 2004). In Chapters 4 and 5, the urban infrastructures—as the Foucauldian "apparatus of governmentality"—reveal forms of political rationality that underline technological projects (Foucault, 2010, p. 70).

Shin believes that "Asian states had been committing to the economic development for decades while maintaining authoritarian, non-democratic governance systems to quell opposition voices that would hinder economic pursuit" (Shin, 2019, p. 6). Pow suggests that such an authoritarian nature of urban governance accompanying the success of urban development among leading Asian economies is what makes the Asian models sought after by the urban elites of the Global South (Pow, 2014, p. 300). In this vein, researching materialities of infrastructure will help us to understand the ideological and discursive dimensions of infrastructure in specific sociopolitical contexts. Meanwhile, discussing a form of infrastructure is a "categorical act", because "it comprises a cultural analytic that high-lights the epistemological and political commitments involved in se-lecting what one sees an infrastructural (and thus causal) and what one leaves out" (Larkin, 2013, p. 330). Based on the World Economic Forum Global Competitiveness report in terms of infrastructure ca-pabilities, South Asia is currently one of the most dynamic regions in the world.[1] Yet, according to World Bank Group's policy research group's reports,[2] the South Asia region is home to the largest pool of individuals living under the poverty line, coupled with a fast-growing population. As well, the region's rates of access to infrastructure (sanitation, electricity, telecom and transport) are closer to those of Sub-Saharan Africa, the one exception being water, where the South Asia region is comparable to East Asia and the Pacific and Latin America and the Caribbean. At the same time, South Asia region features significant heterogeneities within and among countries in terms of access to infrastructure services. In addition, over the past two decades, although the burst of economic growth has generated additional revenue and increased fiscal space to shift more funds to infrastructure, it has also put immense pressure on demands for in-frastructure (Biller et al., 2014). In the case of Malaysia, as will be discussed thoroughly in Chapters 4 and 5, since the 1990s, the coun-try has followed the main precepts of neo-liberalism and gradually privatised the necessary urban services.

Apart from the emphasis on materialities of infrastructure, Simone proposes an idea of "people as infrastructure", conjunctions of ob-jects, spaces, practices and interpersonal relationships in which peo-ple engage to produce and reproduce lives in cities (Simone, 2004). So, the study of the infrastructures might centre on built things and knowledge things or people things (Larkin, 2013, p. 329). Similarly, Foucault and Bourdieu's studies focused on the necessity of analysing ordinary people's everyday lives as forms of resistance. According to Foucault, "the state is super-structural in relation to a whole series of power networks that invest the body, sexuality, the family, kinship, knowledge, technology and so forth" (Foucault, 1980, p. 123). In this definition, the state relies for support on these localised relations of power. Because each individual is subject to power relations at the daily encounter, each individual is subjected to power relations. In constructing a theory of power, Bourdieu tries "to specify in theo-retical terms the processes whereby, in all societies, order and social restraints are produced by indirect, cultural mechanisms rather than by direct and coercive social control" (Jenkins, 1992, p. 104).

Inclusion/exclusion: boundary objects

"The truth is the whole. The whole, however, is merely the essential nature reaching its completeness through the process of its own development" (Hegel, 2005, p. 81).

Focusing on the idea of radical inclusivity in the first chapter, this section aims to conceptualise the notion of inclusion/exclusion through the lens of Hegelian triad model, which paves the way to introduce the boundary object's theoretical framework or the concept of exclusion. Hegelian triad is built upon the dialectics of Aufhebung, according to which oppositional elements, in the forms of thesis and antithesis, engage in a struggle with each other. Hegel's model provides continual dialectical development, which leads ultimately to the fulfilment of the absolute spirit (Pang, 2016, p. 109).

Comparing to the 'Hegelian triad', Marxist dialectics is all about the contradictions. In the Marxist traditions, Mao's theory of dialectic— which is dialectically structured both in form and in content—seems to be slightly subtler (probably unconsciously influenced by Taoism). It begins by affirming the universality of contradiction, then it affirms the particularity of contradiction and concludes with the dialectic of contradiction (Soo, 1981, p. 115). In this sense, the current shape of the Chinese state was firmly influenced by a discussion on dialectic from 1964. In the case of China, in particular, Weber's study of the interplay of orthodoxy (Confucianism) and heterodoxy (Taoism) remains merely descriptive because of his refusal to see society in terms of social classes (Freiberg, 1977).

Reading Hegel from the universalist perspective (we can call it 'Absolute') any activity is imperfect because it is fragmented. This distant horizon of the whole is a totality, but because it is 'out there', it is transcendent to this world. It also prevents any totalitarian claim. In this interpretation, universalist interpretation of Hegel's thought leads us towards an idea of radical inclusivity.

Jeff Carreira, in his book, represents the notion of radical inclusivity as an experience of "nondual consciousness that occurs when the duality between inside and outside collapses" (Carreira, 2014, p. 10). In the face of adversity, the sense of community is reborn together with a selfless impulse to help. So, 'empathy' and 'inclusiveness' become keywords. In this sense, radically inclusive architecture is then a program of revolutionary change aiming to free the architecture form the clutches of the neoliberal paradigm and the logic of short-term profit (Nawratek and Nawratek, 2015, p. 22). However, Yusof and Kozlowski believe that as the result of neoliberal policies urban design has been gradually shifting from a universal discipline aimed at developing urban inclusivity and creating places for all people to a master planning tool delivering new urban enclaves characterised by exclusionary qualities (Yusof and Kozlowski, 2015, p. 81).

The idea of inclusivity is directly connected with the notion of the boundary/shared space or the concept of exclusion (Tonkiss, 2015, p. 172). This research follows Susan Leigh Star's conceptual work on the notion of 'boundary objects' as an arrangement that allows different groups to work together without prior consensus (Star, 2010). So, we see urban space/urban infrastructure as "boundary objects", defined by Susan Leigh Star (2010) as ".... a sort of arrangement that allows different groups to work together without consensus". In better words, boundary objects as the mechanism of intersection are similar enough to serve as a focus for exchange. In Chapter 5, the performance of existing urban and social infrastructures against a set of recognised principles and best practices for sustainable and inclusive infrastructure will be analysed in detail. For conceptualising the relationship between citizens and the socio-spatial infrastructure of the city, the social facilities being currently built in KLMR will be discussed further in Chapter 5. However, it is important to note that by redefining the intercultural dialogues as the boundary encounters, we often require effort to develop concepts understood by the participants; however, the theory of boundary objects can make the process clearer.

One dominant way to think of infrastructures is as a "system of substrates" that underlies the built phenomenal world such as pipes, cables, sewers and wires (Star, 1999, p. 380). However, "analytically, infrastructure appears only as a relational property, not as a thing stripped of use" (Star and Ruhleder, 1996, p. 113). Simultaneously, they are used and interpreted by members of different communities. Even before achieving consensus, 'boundary objects' play a critical role by allowing members of different groups to find common ground and work together (Leeds-Hurwitz, 2014).

Boundary objects are not useful at just any level of scale or without full consideration of the entire model (Star, 2010, p. 601). According to Susan Leigh Start: "boundary objects are material and at the same time affect a process, their meaning is open to various interpretations, they are based in action, subject to reflection and local tailoring, and their meaning may develop while being used" (Star, 2010).

Focusing on 'architecture of boundary objects' Leigh Star introduced three dimensions. First, there is the aspect of interpretive flexibility, which is hardly new in philosophy or history. However, she added that there are two other aspects of boundary objects that are rarely used, including the material/organizational structure of different types of boundary objects and the question of scale/granularity (Star, 2010, p. 602). In this sense, boundary objects are

> plastic enough to adapt to the needs and constraints of the several parties that employ them, yet robust enough to maintain identity ... They have different meanings in different social worlds, but their structure is common enough to more than one world to make them recognizable, a means of translation.
>
> (Star and Griesemer, 1989, p. 393)

Discussions of boundary objects evoke the concept of 'marginality' since it exists at the intersection of two (or more) disparate social worlds without fully belonging to any of them (Star and Griesemer, 1989, p. 411). In this interpretation, for understanding the various actors involved in complex situations, boundary objects introduce a lens to help us to understand the situation despite having different and conflicting interests. As well, looking at complex conditions through the lens of boundary objects can help us to understand how the various actors involved can cooperate on a project. The next section will introduce the idea of Community—it has already been discussed in the first chapter—as inclusive infrastructure through Ernesto Laclau's theorization of the empty signifier.

Empty signifier: community as inclusive infrastructure

> The truth is the whole. An empty signifier can, consequently, only emerge if there is a structural impossibility in signification as such, and only if this impossibility can signify itself as an interruption (subversion, distortion, etcetera) of the structure of the sign.
>
> (Laclau, 1996b)

As it has already been analysed in the first chapter, the community assumes a standard set of features that distinguish members of the community from those who are outside. This section aims to theorise the community as a semi-transcendent mechanism (inclusive infrastructure) allowing diverse subjects to execute their agency. In the context of this study, the community defines as "empty signifier" (Ernesto Laclau)—its understanding and the way how it is actualised is open to interpretation by its members and how it is associated with the concept of universality. Laclau believes that the empty signifier is the product of the 'exclusionary limit' of a signifying system through distinct effects such as 'ambivalence' and 'negativity'. Therefore, these effects "introduce an essential ambivalence within the system of differences" (Laclau, 1996, p. 38).

The above-mentioned 'system of differences' reasserts ideational accounts through the application of the political discourse theory of Laclau and Mouffe. This approach posits ideas in governing discourses to be able to understand how general equivalent demands then become empty signifiers. Therefore, an empty signifier arises out of a specific political process in which a particular statement, signifier or practice is transformed into a universality (Wullweber, 2015, p. 80). Such organ-less bodies are all made up of a multitude of individuals that can act quite effectively as a mass without any centralised leadership (Mehan and Rossi, 2019, p. 240). Women identity has been explored as one example of the types of political groupings and organ-less bodies described by Ernesto Laclau and Chantal Mouffe in Hegemony and Socialist Strategy (Mehan, 2017, p. 88). According to Laclau, this political process is conceptualised as a hegemonic operation:

> No social fullness is achievable except through hegemony; and hegemony is nothing more than the investment, in a partial object, of fullness which will always evade because it is purely mythical.
>
> (Laclau, 2005, p. 116)

Following this definition, it is a task for the protagonists of a particular empty signifier to strengthen the relation to the hegemonic common good within the discourse of interest (Wullweber, 2015, p. 91). Based on Laclau's definition, groups are constituted through a double process, which establishes a chain of equivalences that obliterates the differences within, and an antagonistic boundary defining their limits (Laclau, 1996). Therefore, "the differential character of social identities collapses as they become inscribed in chains of equivalence that construct them in terms of a certain 'sameness'" (Torfing, 1999, p. 124). The empty signifier represents the impossible identity of the community. According to Laclau and Mouffe, establishing a discourse is to "dominate the field of discursivity, to arrest the flow of differences, to construct a centre" (Laclau and Mouffe, 2005, pp. 7–91).

Major findings

In the section, the community is (constitutes by a specific nodal point) defined as an empty signifier that allows different elements to associate in a relation of equivalence and represents an antagonistic boundary defining their limits such as excluding the fundamentally different "other". Following the empty signifier theoretical framework, community is defined as the discursive element that has been emptied of its actual content and provides for the unity of the discourse. However, the problem with the community lies in its totality and unification—the community assumes a common set of features that distinguish members of the community from those who are outside. But each of these features includes (however small) mechanism of inclusion—this mechanism not only allows any community to expand, but it also prevents the community against total unification. This 'inclusive remnants' (metaphorically could be defined as a 'free inclusive radicals') could be amplified to break through the community itself and to become the elements of 'inclusive infrastructure', not creating a community but building the commons.

Thus, entities and structures can also be imposed by specific actors that have primarily been established by political acts of hegemonic closure. The construction of this hegemonic closure presupposes the exclusion of individual elements as the radical others. These radical others can simply define those elements that are not part of the system. Considering this outside/inside dichotomy, this section suggests that the social entities have the potential ability to 'do' social action. As Abbott puts it 'Action can be seen as 'an ability to create an effect on the rest of the social process that goes beyond effects that are merely transmitted through the causing entity from elsewhere' (Abbott, 1995, p. 873).

Note

1 They can be divided into two broad categories: physical and economic infrastructure, which includes railways, roads, airports, ports, energy systems, telecommunications, water supply, drainage and sewerage systems, and social infrastructure, which includes housing, health and education facilities. For more readings about the physical and economic infrastructures, see L. Hardwicke, 2008. "Transition to Smart, Sustainable Infrastructure." In *Transitions: Pathway Towards Sustainable Urban Development in Australia*, by Peter W. Newton, 599–608.

Bibliography

Abbott, A. (1995) Things of Boundaries. *Social Research: An International Quarterly*, 63(1), 857–882.

Biller, D., Andres, L., and Dappe, M. H. (2014) Infrastructure Gap in South Asia: Inequality of Access to Infrastructure Services. *Policy Research Working Paper 7033.* https://openknowledge.worldbank.org/bitstream/handle/10986/20344/WPS7033.pdf?sequence=1&isAllowed=y

Buchanan, I. (2000) Strategies and Tactics. In: I. Buchanan, ed. *Michel de Certeau: Cultural Theorist.* London: SAGE Publications, pp. 86–107.

Bunnell, T. (2017) Introduction: Futurity and Urban Asia. In: T. Bunnell and D. P. S. Goh, eds. *Urban Asias: Essays on Futurity Past and Present.* Berlin: Jovis, pp. 9–20.

Carreira, J. (2014) *Radical Inclusivity: Expanding Our Minds Beyond Dualistic Thinking.* Philadelphia, PA: Emergence Education & Jeff Carreira.

Choguill, L. C. (1996) Ten Steps to Sustainable Infrastructure. *Habitat International*, 20(3), 389–404.

Corey, K. E. (2004) Moving People, Goods, and Information in Singapore: Intelligent Corridors. In: R. E. Hanley, ed. *Moving People, Goods, and Information in the 21st Century: The Cutting-Edge Infrastructure of Networked Cities.* London: Routledge, pp. 323–358.

de Certeau, M. (1984) *The Practice of Everyday Life.* S. Rendall, trans. and ed. Berkeley, CA: University of California Press.

Doucette, J., and Park, B.-G. (2018) Urban Developmentalism in East Asia: Geopolitical Economies, Spaces of Exception, and Networks of Expertise. *Critical Sociology*, 44(3), 395–403.

Foucault, M. (1980) Truth and Power. In: C. Gordon, ed. *Power/Knowledge: Selected Interviews and Other Writings, 1972–1977.* New York: Random House, pp. 109–133.

Foucault, M. (2010) *The Birth of Biopolitics: Lectures at the College de France, 1978–1979.* New York: Picador.

Freiberg, J. W. (1977) The Dialectic of Confucianism and Taoism in Ancient China. *Dialectical Anthropology*, 2, doi:10.1007/bf00249484

Graham, S., and Marvin, S. (2001) *Splintering Urbanism: Networked Infrastructures, Technological Mobilities and the Urban Condition.* London: Routledge.

Hardwicke, L. (2008) Transition to Smart, Sustainable Infrastructure. In: P. W. Newton, ed. *Transitions: Pathway Towards Sustainable Urban Development in Australia.* Clayton: CSIRO Publishing, pp. 599–608.

Hegel, G. W. F. (2005) *The Phenomenology of Mind.* New York: Cosimo Classics.

Jenkins, R. (1992) *Pierre Bourdieu.* London and New York: Routledge.

Jullien, F. (1995) *The Propensity of Things: Toward a History of Efficacy in China.* New York: Zone Books.

Laclau, E. (1996a) *Emancipation(s).* London and New York: Verso.

Laclau, E. (1996b) Why Do Empty Signifiers Matter to Politics? In: E. Laclau, ed. *Emancipation(s).* London and New York: Verso, pp. 36–46.

Laclau, E. (2005) *On Populist Reason.* London: Verso.

Laclau, E., and Mouffe, C. (2005) *Hegemony and Socialist Strategy: Towards a Radical Democratic Politics.* London: Verso.

Larkin, B. (2013) The Politics and Poetics of Infrastructure. *Annual Review of Anthropology,* 42(1), 327–343.

Leeds-Hurwitz, W. (2014) Boundary Objects. *Key Concepts in Intercultural Dialogue.* http://centerforinterculturaldialogue.files.wordpress.com/2014/10/key-concept-boundary-objects.pdf.

Lefebvre, H. (1991) *The Production of Space.* Oxford: Blackwell.

Massey, D. (1999) Spaces of Politics. In: J. Allen and P. Sarre, eds. *Human Geography Today.* Cambridge: Polity Press, pp. 279–294.

Mehan, A. (2017) Review of "The Empty Place: Democracy and Public Space" by Teresa Hoskyns. *ID: International Dialogue, A Multidisciplinary Journal of World Affairs,* 7, 86–90.

Mehan, A., and Rossi, U. (2019) Multiplying Resistance: The Power of the Urban in the Age of National Revanchism. In: J. Malpas and K. Jacobs, eds. *Philosophy and the City: Interdisciplinary and Transcultural Perspectives.* London and New York: Rowman & Littlefield International, pp. 233–245.

Nawratek, K., and Nawratek, K. (2015) On the Frustrating Impossibility of Inclusive Architecture. In: K. J. Nawratek, ed. *Radical Inclusivity: Architecture and Urbanism.* Barcelona: dpr-barcelona, pp. 12–23.

Ooi, G. L. (2005) *Sustainability and Cities: Concept and Assessment.* Singapore: Institute of Policy Studies.

Pang, L. (2016) Mao's Dialectical Materialism: Possibilities for the Future. *Rethinking Marxism: A Journal of Economics, Culture & Society,* 28(1), 108–123.

Pow, C. P. (2014) License to Travel: Policy Assemblage and the 'Singapore Model'. *City,* 18(3), 287–306.

Schindler, S. (2017) Towards a Paradigm of Southern Urbanism. *City,* 21(1), 47–64.

Shin, H. B. (2019) Asian Urbanism. In: A.M. Orum, ed. *The Wiley-Blackwell Encyclopedia of Urban and Regional Studies.* London: Wiley-Blackwell. http://eprints.lse.ac.uk/91490/1/Shin_Asian-urbanism.pdf.

Simone, A. (2004) People as Infrastructure: Intersecting Fragments in Johannesburg. *Public Culture,* 16(3), 407–429.

Soo, F. Y. K. (1981) *Mao Tse-Tung's Theory of Dialectic.* Boston: D. Reidel Publishing Company.

Star, S. L. (1999) The Ethnography of Infrastructure. *American Behavioral Scientist,* 43(3), 377–391.

Star, S. L. (2010) This Is Not a Boundary Object: Reflections on the Origin of a Concept. *Science, Technology, & Human Values,* 35(5), 601–617.

Star, S. L., and Griesemer, J. R. (1989) Institutional Ecology, 'Translations' and Boundary Objects: Amateurs and Professionals in Berkeley's Museum of Vertebrate Zoology, 1907–39. *Social Studies of Science,* 19(3), 387–420.

Star, S. L., and Ruhleder, K. (1996) Steps Toward an Ecology of Infrastructure: Design and Access for Large Information Spaces. *Information Systems Research*, 1(7), 111–135.

Tonkiss, F. (2015) Interview. In: K. Nawratek, ed. *Radical Inclusivity: Architecture and Urbanism*. Barcelona: dpr-barcelona, pp. 172–178.

Torfing, J. (1999) *New Theories of Discourse: Laclau, Mouffe and Žižek*. Oxford: Blackwell Publishers Ltd.

Wullweber, J. (2015) Global Politics and Empty Signifiers: The Political Construction of High Technology. *Critical Policy Studies*, 9(1), 78–96.

Yusof, Y. M., and Kozlowski, M. (2015) Clients of Contemporary Urban Design: The Impact of Neoliberalism. In: *Radical Inclusivity: Architecture and Urbanism*. Barcelona: dpr-barcelona, pp. 76–110.

3   National unity and urban segregation

Introduction

Kuala Lumpur (KL) is a city in which representatives of different religions and nationalities live together. However, since the 1970s, policies have favoured the Bumiputra (which means 'son of the soil') group comprising mainly Malays as an attempt to improve their living standards and narrow the wide gap between the more affluent urban Chinese population and the impoverished Malays deriving from rural areas. The recent and the previous government have been actively promoting national unity and cohesion through a program called '1Malaysia', but the detailed legal regulations still give preference to the Malay majority. This chapter presents the ideological and legal framework of national unity and explores if there are any practices of urban segregation in the Kuala Lumpur Metropolitan Region (KLMR)—based on differences in economic status, ethnicity and religion.

Current ethnic division

KL with its urban agglomeration KLMR is a multi-ethnic and multi-religious megacity. There are four main religions in KL: Muslim (46.4%), Buddhist (35.7%), Hindu (8.5%) and Christian (5.8%) (World Population Review, 2019). The history of KL starts in the 19th century, as a mining settlement inhabited mostly by Chinese workers. Over the last 150 years, the demographic composition changed, but the Chinese population is still significant (slightly more than 40%), roughly similar to the Malay population (World Population Review, 2019). For years, intense tensions between the Malay and Chinese communities have been built; it was in the Vision 2020 speech that Dr Mahathir introduced the concept of "Bangsa Malaysia" (Malaysian race):

This must be a nation at peace with itself, territorially and ethnically integrated, living in harmony and full and fair partnership made up of one "Bangsa Malaysia" with political loyalty and dedication to the nation. (Mahathir Mohamad, 1991; quoted: Saad, S. (2012). Re-building the concept of nation-building in Malaysia. *Asian Social Science*, 8(4), 115.) The various ethnic oriented policies within Malaysia draw a sharp contrast with the rhetoric of Bangsa Malaysia and 1Malaysia as described in the words of Dr Mahathir and one of his successors, the former Prime Minister Najib Razak, respectively. According to Fujita (2010), a nation that gives special provisions to one group (particularly the majority group) over others is not one in which people are living in harmony and fair partnership. While both Bangsa Malaysia and 1Malaysia attempt to put forth an image of unity and solidarity, the image is a thin veneer peeling back at the edges to expose an internal struggle for identity.

The new government elected in 2018 and led again by Dr Mahathir seems to change the tune and genuinely aim to build bridges between diverse Malaysian communities. However, this new direction suffered a setback when under pressure from Malay groups, the government had to withdraw from ratifying International Convention on the Elimination of all Forms of Racism and Discrimination (ICERD).

It is worth to be mentioned that in Malaysia as a whole the percentage of Malays is slightly higher and is around 51% with the Bumiputera population of 67% (Department of Statistics Malaysia, 2019). This makes KL, capital of Malaysia with 45% of Malay/Bumiputra, a slightly less 'Malay' city than the country itself; however, other cities in the KLMR have a higher percentage of Malay population, with the administrative capital of Putrajaya having 97% of its population Malay, making it almost an exclusive Malay enclave (City Population Putrajaya, 2019). What makes KL distinct is the high percentage of the Chinese population, which at 40% is significantly higher than the national average percentage of 25% (Department of Statistics, Malaysia, 2019). The policy adopted by the Malaysian government creates apparent cultural, social and political tensions, sometimes visible in urban spaces of the city. According to the Chinese community representatives, there is a pressure to diminish the Chinese history of the city, mostly by ignoring Chinese historical figures and changing historical Chinese names. One of the examples of the fight to preserve the Chinese history of the city is a story of Petaling Street and also controversies around Chinese cemeteries (Yat Ming, 2016).

Diminishing Chinese history can be traced back to the physical urban environment. KL until today does not have any policies protecting the traditional Chinese shop-houses, and as a result, a significant number of these buildings came under the hammer to pave the way for new development.

In this context particularly interesting is a discussion about the creation of Chinatown in KL around Petaling Street:

> ......'Chinatown' in KL has its colonial roots as an 'Other' space, in line with the spatial segregation of the Chinese from other races (Yat Ming, 2012). While the prestigious Kuala Lumpur City Centre (KLCC) development symbolised the new power corporate Malaysia and the state and the Malay elites, the original Chinese neighbourhood near Petaling Street was converted into a 'Chinatown' and confined as a minority and marginal urban space. Lacking participation in the state's nation-building architectural and urban projects, the Chinese were left to preserve their own version of history and their cultural heritage sites in Kuala Lumpur.
>
> (Yat Ming, 2012)

The mechanism of marginalisation of the ethnic group, which historically has been the most important in KL and is still extremely important as an economic actor, proves that nationalistic policies of Malaysian governments are controversial. The tensions between top-down, state-driven, Malay-focused policies and bottom-up initiatives are interesting, also when analyses of local civic activists groups focused on the improvement of the quality of life in KL. One of the most exciting and triumphant stories of this sort is The Bicycle Map Project (The Guardian, 2015), which cannot be assigned to one ethnicity, but at the same moment, Chinese activist should be seen as critical actors in starting and then successfully developing this project.

National legal framework: implications on the urban environment

Malaysia constitution and legal system make a distinction based on ethnicity (on Bumiputera, the 'original inhabitants'—mostly Malays— and others) and based on religion—Islam and other. There is an ongoing discussion on the position of Islam in Malaysia. The constitution declares that Islam is a religion of the Malaysian Federation. However, it is not clear what the legal consequences of this statement are. One of them is considerable difficulty in converting from Islam to any other religion. In general, however, the constitution is ambiguous, it does not declare Malaysia as an Islamic state, but it does not declare it as a secular state either. However, the presence of Islamic jurisdiction plays a hugely significant role in Malaysia, just because all Muslim citizens are scrutinised under the sharia concerning civil law (Sharia Law does not apply to criminal offences). It creates a strange parallel legal system—different for Muslim citizens and different for everybody else. The foundations of today's political system in Malaysia are still based on the New Economic Policy (NEP) introduced in the early 1970s. NEP had two pillars: one was to eradicate poverty and the other was an affirmative action policy for the Bumiputra to achieve 30% of the corporate wealth by the 1990s (Lim, 2017).

Religious segregation causes spatial segregation—in part concerning places where different ethnic and religious groups live and in part concerning the way how urban spaces are used: religions, especially Islam, shape significantly lifestyles of believers. There are several layers of how one can analyse these religious-spatial differences. On the basic level, one can see elements of religious infrastructure—places where believers of different religions pray, places where they eat (for example, restaurants serving halal food versus restaurants serving pork), to some extent also places where customers do shopping—there are separated enclaves where one can buy non-halal food and alcoholic drinks. The segregation is strict in some places, but then there are also places where the territory of different religious groups overlap, mostly in major public spaces, corner small eating places or in shopping malls. Also, the general public transport infrastructure is used equally by diverse groups.

Kozlowski (2014) argues that any new visitor to Malaysia will notice distinctive roles for each ethnic community in the country; the Malays are in charge of administration, while the Chinese and the Indians are predominant in commerce. This phenomenon is clearly visible in the KL agglomeration where the Chinese were and are still playing a leading role in the urban economy, with major developers including Setia, YTL and IOI all being in the hands of powerful Chinese lobby groups. On the other side, all local governments, including local political positions and the entire civil service, are totally dominated by the Malays.

The ethnic divisions observed until today in Malaysia derive mostly from the 1948 Federation of Malaya Agreement, which was created by the British in alliance with United Malays National Organisation (UMNO) (the main Malay political movement) partly because of

British fears of the rapidly growing involvement of the Chinese population in the communist insurgency. The Malaysian constitution and the Malaysian state were born during the Cold War environment of the 1950s, where British concerns regarding Chinese communist infiltration were the significant determinants behind any decision making. After independence, the Federal Government has undertaken affirmative action targeting the political and administrative systems. As a result, in a diverse, multicultural community, one ethnic group (the Bumiputra) controls practically all positions in the judiciary, public administrative organs, the police, armed forces and the public universities. This affirmative action can be labelled as ethnocracy, giving one ethnic group the exclusivity of governance and decision making (Wade, 2014). After the 2018 elections, the new Pakatan Harapan Government has challenged ethnocracy by appointing members of other ethnic groups to critical political and administrative positions. However, this new approach has already received criticism and backlash from the Malay majority. Ethnocracy has left a visible mark on the urban and architectural form of major Malaysian cities, including the KLMR.

However, the Chinese community in Malaysia retained most of their freedoms and privileges, allowing in preserving their culture, language and original names. Major shopping centres are fully decorated during major Chinese festivities such as Chinese New Year or the Chinese Moon Cake Festival, and Chinese public schools are still sponsored by the Federal Government. The strong presence of Chinese culture in KL is clearly visible to any new visitor to Malaysia. Despite ethnic tensions, the situation never reached the level of that in Indonesia where under the new "'Order Policies' of the Suharto regime Chinese Indonesians were forced to adopt Indonesian names" (South China Morning Post, 2017).

This book mostly focuses on interactions between three main ethnic groups practising four main religions, but one must be aware that KL as a global city has an exceptionally diverse population, including (mostly Western) expats and (primarily Asian) immigrants. The distinction between expats and immigrants has a potentially racist and positively colonial taste; it is used here not to reinforce the colonial narrative but to make clear about its existence. The expat community is in general relatively detached from the majority of Malaysian society and occupies in general economically better-off spheres. It is visible when analysing mobility patterns (Butler and Hannam, 2014) of expats, heavily relying on private cars. The other means of transport, especially public transport, are seen as exceptions, and their value lay more in social and cultural experiences than in transport itself

...we argue that public modes of transportation may also play pivotal roles in enabling expatriates to achieve a number of new experiential demands. Trains acted as viable platforms for a number of sensecapes to be encountered that represented the socially constructed real Malaysia for expatriates.

(Butler and Hannam, 2014)

The diversity of KL residents could be seen while analysing language signs and adverts present in the urban space. The most surprising fact seems to be that English remains a language to integrate diverse parts of Malaysian society. It is probably not seen anymore as a language of colonial oppressors and has become a 'semi-neutral' language transcendent to tensions and conflicts existing in Malaysian society:

The data as a whole indicate that the number of monolingual signs is comparatively much lower (10%) than bilingual (41%) and multilingual signs (49%). The English language appears on 71.82% monolingual signs, whereas Bahasa Melayu (Malay Language) stands second with 17.1%. The other languages marginally appearing on monolingual signs include Mandarin, Arabic and Myanmar.

(Manan et al., 2015)

English is seen as a 'global language', allowing Malaysians to plug-in into global flows of knowledge, information and financial exchanges.

Transportation patterns differ between different ethnic and social groups. Interestingly, these differences could also be seen in an attitude to walking:

A comparison of the walking behaviour levels between different ethnic groups found that only 18.9% of Chinese, 37.9% of Malays, and 49.7% of Indian respondents reached the recommended level for walking activity per week to gain any health benefits. When comparing different purposes of walking, the majority of Indians and Chinese mainly walked for transport purposes (approximately 55 and 30 minutes, respectively) while the Malays walked for recreation (approximately 43 minutes).

(Wan et al., 2013)

A survey based on observations, while walking from the city edge to the city centre, was conducted in 2017. The exercise included a journey by bus or train to the last available stop followed by a stroll back to central KL. This exercise could be seen partly as a remnant of situationist practice of urban drifting, somewhat weird kind of urban tourism and partly a personal spiritual experience. This was a great way to understand the spatial diversity of KL, where high-rises and dense urban structures dot fragments of the semi-rural landscape. It was also an excellent opportunity to understand why walking in KL is so unpopular. There is nothing in the city to support this means of transport. The system of pedestrian routes is patchy; high temperature and humidity make the whole experience highly unpleasant. The understanding of 'pedestrian unfriendliness' of KL also helps to understand the specificity of urban open public spaces in the city. The public spaces are in general used by diverse ethnic and religious groups, and it is not uncommon to observe multi-ethnic and multi-religious groups on squares or in restaurants. The biggest challenge to researchers is to define where these groups are formed. It seems almost impossible to observe any process of social interactions between strangers in public spaces. There are invisible social barriers, mostly created by religious and cultural factors preventing strangers of a different sex to attempt to interact in an open space. The public space in KL cannot be defined as a space of random encounters, and it should be questioned to what extent the very idea of public space as a Western (European) political and cultural construct is relevant to define spaces in KL. In general, this book argues against the conventional narrative of public open spaces, presented, for example, by Amir and Soha (2019). They adopt the western perspective to discuss areas in KL as a local variation of the global phenomenon. Our approach is drastically different. For example, when Amir and Soha describe (responsible) public space, they say that one of the factors that determine it is 'cleanness'. From the perspective of this study, any attempt to define the aesthetic quality of the space has exclusive power. By definition, 'clean' space excludes particular groups of potential users because of activities (leisure or work-related) they are engaged with. The interest in public spaces lies in their accessibility and ability to integrate different ethnic and religious groups or at least to support some interactions between members of different communities. One of the most significant factors preventing this is deep suspicion among the Muslim population of interaction between non-related people of different sex in a public space.

Religion, as stated before, could be a significant factor blocking interactions between members of different communities. However, it is worth to mention that some deep spiritual foundation could be seen across the whole Malaysian society. This book focuses on three main ethnic groups having four different religions. While Malays are predominantly Muslim, religious identity in Chinese and Indian communities is more diverse and complex. Members of these ethnicities may identify themselves as Hindu, Buddhists, Christians, Sikh and also Muslim.

Interestingly, the Pentecostal movement (one of the most rapidly growing denomination in Christianity) has its World Congress in KL in 2013. Pentecostal churches are growing mostly in Africa and Latin America (mainly in Brazil). From the perspective of this book, this phenomenon could be more significant than expected. If Kay (2013) is right saying

> ...Pentecostalism thrives in cultures where its own view engages the predominant worldview of a country or region (Freston, 1998, 2004; Anderson, 2004). Where belief in spirits is prevalent, and the majority worldview is largely unaffected by the results of the western enlightenment, Pentecostalism offers a powerful protective belief in the work of the Holy Spirit as an antidote to the contingent malignancy of evil forces or ancestral influences.
>
> (Kay, 2013)

Pentecostalism may be seen as a postmodern type of Christianity. In a context of KL, the growth of Pentecostalism should be seen as a sign of a profoundly spiritual and enchanted, anti-enlightenment foundations of Malaysian (or at least Chinese–Malaysian) society. This deep spirituality also influences more architecture-related decisions. One excellent example is the importance in an attitude towards fengshui:

> Many Malaysian Chinese still consider fengshui as one of the criteria in buying a house, other than housing price and property location. Their perceptions on the influence of fengshui factors will affect their house buying intentions, and hence the selection of property sites for development by property developers in terms of the surrounding environment and external layout, as well as design of houses by architects in terms internal layout and interior arrangement.
>
> (Sia et al., 2018)

The tensions between different ethnic groups are also seen in more public elements of the city. Interestingly, the central axis of tension lies between Malays and Chinese, while the interests of other groups, mainly Indian, are strangely absent. The history of Malaysian architecture since the independence evolves from inclusive nationalism and vernacularism to a version of pan-Islamism and finally to globalism.

> In the case of the National Mosque, its significance is inevitable: it is the first national showcase of Malay-Islamic identity. The National Mosque is noted for its modernist architectural spirit which incorporated features from the traditional Malay house such as the pitched roof (symbolised by the umbrella-like roof) and serambi spaces (or verandah galleries).
>
> (Kien, 2005)

> Further tropical features evidenced by terrazzo-grilled screens on three sides of the buildings served to protect and keep internal spaces cool. (…) It is clear that there has been an aphoristic shift in Malaysian architecture toward the 2000s with the arrival of paradigms characterised by direct borrowings from Middle-Eastern and colonial architecture to symbolise an Islamic national identity. When compared to Independence architectural efforts which were marked by more locally relevant modernist architectural models, the rise of Middle-Eastern architecture in KL and Putrajaya has fundamentally overturned the former ethic.
>
> (Goh and Liauw, 2009)

The pinnacle of Middle Eastern architecture is demonstrated in Putrajaya, the new administrative capital located between KL and Kuala Lumpur International Airport (KLIA). Putrajaya built by the federal government portrays an image of strong legislative, judicial and executive powers giving a boost and popularity to the ruling political establishment. The ruling political establishment being predominantly Malay opted for an administrative capital that will symbolise Pan Malay and Pan Islamic styles that would transmit a strong image to the rest of the World of new-born Malaysia's Middle Eastern expression. Therefore, the first government buildings in Putrajaya, including the main Putra Mosque, were built in an architectural style imported from Isfahan in Iran with other elements of the building being replicas of mosques in Iraq, Morocco and Egypt (Bunnell, 2014, Kozlowski, 2014).

This shift from seeking a national, Malaysian style into mostly following Middle-Eastern aesthetic seems to lose its momentum in the 21st century. Contemporary Malaysian architecture is more global and less local. However, there are also several inspiring examples of a new, deeply rooted in a language of tropical modernism, architecture.

This new architectural language in general attempts to be more universal—not only it refers to global architectural trends, but it is also stronger contextualised in particular locations in Malaysia. References are less cultural and more climatic. If designed architecture could be a sign of more profound national reconciliation and unification, contemporary Malaysian architecture may be seen as a promise of a better, more inclusive city for (almost all) its residents. The recent predominant architectural styles include abstract regionalism where the aim is to 'evoke' the vernacular rather than inserting traditional vernacular forms. The champions of abstract regionalism include Malaysia's leading architects such as Ken Yeang and Hijjas Kasturi (Kassim et al., 2017).

In this chapter, the problem of migrant minority groups is briefly addressed. One of them is the migrant workers, who constitute almost 9% of KL's population. This is a transient community, and it is not only present in the city but also actively transferring its landscape:

> At one end of Jalan Silang is a small shopping mall, which also has a very busy bus terminal on the intersection. This particular street is the heart of the Bangladeshi, Nepali and Burmese migrant communities in the city. (…) During my visits to Jalan Silang, I was immediately struck by just how profoundly this urban space has been transformed over a relatively short period of time. What used to be a collection of mostly Chinese businesses has now been replaced by entirely different and new ones; Bollywood/South Asian entertainment stores, Bangladeshi and Burmese cuisine restaurants, money-transfer agents, phone and prepaid vendors and South Asian textile/garment retail stores.
>
> (Muniandy, 2015)

However, apart from increasing ethnic and cultural diversity, the paternalistic culture is present strongly in KL and among migrants.

> Migrant women are barely present in public areas such as sidewalks and streets, largely confined to working indoors as cooks, servers, cleaners and sex-workers. (…) The visible (public) presence of male migrants and the submergence of both women's physical presence and labour in districts such as these are largely a consequence of broader transnational gendering of migrant labour. Women have been, and continue to be, moved into types of work that have traditionally been gendered as 'feminine', which in contexts like Malaysia implies domesticity and the private sphere (the family).
>
> (Muniandy, 2015)

Today, KL is a megacity, spreading across a vast area. Its population is increasingly diverse, making KL another global city, closely connected to international networks and becoming increasingly less representative for Malaysia as a whole.

The process of growth has been a combination of market logic and political ambitions, partly related to gerrymandering, partly to big infrastructural projects of regional or national importance and partly because of particular type of identity politics focused on preserving Malay's villages and Malay's traditional style of life ('The Malay Reserve Land'). The Malay Reserve Land was introduced by the British in 1913 to attract rural Malay population to urban areas and also to prevent Malays from being demolished from their own country. Today, Malay Reserve Land areas are still being designated in the KLMR. In Malay Reserve Land areas, ownership can be only exercised by Malays and transferred to other Malays (Sheik Ismail et al., 2016). Based on conducted observations and field survey, the spatial structure of KLMR is then an extremely patchy mixture of highly urbanised areas (residential, industrial and commercial) and (mostly residential) quasi-rural settlements (Kozlowski and Mohd Yusof, 2017). Therefore, the crude socio-spatial distinction is possible to contain Malay and more urban Chinese and Indian populations. Elements of this urban–rural spatial mixture are connected via roads (designed mostly for private users) and different types of railways (designed obviously for public transport). The city operates then according to (at least) three different logics. Spatial structure of urban centres is mostly to develop according to market logic, based on land speculation and financial profit. Despite development pressures, some quasi-rural Malay's villages are protected by law, and its development is regulated and stimulated by political forces. Finally, the transport infrastructure is a hybrid, operating according to the logic of 'basic needs' of the city ('scientific', modernist logic of experts), logic of market (connections between distributed in space and significant economic actors) and philosophy of democratic (but 'contaminated' by sectarian sentiments) politics.

Apart from public transport, KL is serviced by many taxi companies and, over the last couple of years, by private cars operating under Uber and Grab (local Malaysian service) umbrellas.

Urban public space: inclusivity or urban segregation?

The second part of the chapter will look at urban public spaces in the KLMR and determine whether they are open and inclusive to all community groups irrespective of race and religion or whether there is a clear urban segregation.

Shamsuddin (2011) identifies typical human activities taking place in the historic inner-city areas of Malaysian cities. The activities include all trade activities; food-related activities; public activities such as toilets, libraries, post office, medical clinic; religious activities; and all types of leisure, arts and outdoor recreational activities. The author further argues that to take place, all the human activities need associated physical settings and the choice of these activity settings depends on the type of the urban environment. Based on observations and analysis, there are three basic categories of activity settings in the inner-city areas of Malaysia cities:

Medan (square), padang (recreational green field), waterfronts and other open spaces
    Paths such as streets and five-foot ways
    Places such as markets, transportation hubs and shopping malls
(Shamsuddin, 2011)

The central part of KL and inner-city areas of other cities in KL-Klang agglomeration would have the majority of above-mentioned activity settings. Majority of activity settings would be used by all ethnic groups irrespective of race and religions; however, there are some exemptions to this rule.

The padang is a green open space located in the most strategic part of the old town centre. It was used in the colonial days as a sports and recreational node of the town. A padang differs from other open spaces and parks due to its size and formal character and also it lacks trees and other tall vegetation. Its main feature is wide green lawn; therefore, during the British period, padangs were often used for the afternoon cricket sessions. In KL, the former padang has been turned into a formal space called Merdeka Square that accommodates activities such as open-air concerts, parades and state events. It's also often used as a place for demonstrations. Because of its function and purpose, Merdeka Square is open to all ethnic groups and is also a main tourist attraction of the city. However, during government-sponsored events and religious festivities, such as Ramadan, it would be predominantly used by the Malays.

The medans or squares are much less prevalent in Malaysian cities than in European or North American cities. The square (ancient agora in Ancient Greece or forum in Ancient Rome) derives very much from the European urban development culture and appears in the Asian urban environment mainly as an imported urban space element introduced by the colonial powers. In central KL, the typical urban square is Medan Pasar, which is located in the heart of the old town centre. Pasar Medan was the location of the central market place of the town centre back in the late 19th century. The presence of traders and surrounding uses, including gambling booths, opium dens and brothels, contributed to the activity of the place. (Isa and Kaur, 2015). Because of its proximity to Chinatown, it was a predominant Chinese enclave; however, nowadays it is being frequented by all ethnic groups and is also another popular tourist attraction. Medan Pasar, once the bustling node of the city, has lost its importance as a significant public space, with the marketplace being relocated and other businesses shifting to the new commercial nodes located in the eastern part of the city centre.

Stephens et al. (2014) analysing three waterfronts in the KLMR (KLCC artificial lake, River of Life (RoL) corridor between Masjid Jameek and Pasar Seni (the Central Market) and Lake Putrajaya waterfront) argue that all three waterfront landscapes feature generic international ideas without any significant distinct local flavour. The only unique feature along the three waterfronts is the surrounding buildings which in case of KLCC and Putrajaya are a mixture of Pan Islamic, regional vernacular styles and postmodern tropical styles while the RoL corridor is dominated by a combination of historic colonial and universal modernist buildings. In terms of ethnic preferences, waterfronts are open to all groups. The Lake Putrajaya waterfront is mainly used by Malays only because Putrajaya is an exclusive Malay city.

Within the KLMR, there are a significant number of informal places, especially within the inner part of the cities that are occupied by food stalls and used as outdoor eating spaces. The outdoor eating places selling halal food are dominated by the Malays, while the non-halal food outdoor food outlets attract the non-Muslim population. Such informal pocket spaces have become one of the most common activity settings in Malaysian cities (Shamsuddin, 2011).

The central part of KL is flanked by two major parks Taman Tasik Perdana (Lake Gardens) and Taman Titiwangsa. This phenomenon is unique, as the majority of other cities in Malaysia are not surrounded by recreational green open spaces. Both parks feature rich flora and fauna and incorporate lakes as their main attraction (Shamsuddin, 2011). The biggest urban park in central KL is Taman KLCC (KLCC Park). Although KLCC is regarded as a more upmarket exclusive shopping complex, Taman KLCC is accessible to everybody, and during the Hari Raya festivities, it is frequented by Bangladeshi migrant workers. There are two significant natural reserves in KL: Bukit Nanas and Batu Caves. Bukit Nanas is a tropical forest located in the heart of the city and frequented mainly by tourists. Batu Caves located at the north-eastern edge of the city comprises three limestone hills and network of caves. It is the focal point of the Hindu Festival of Taipusam attracting thousands of pilgrims (Kuala Lumpur Attractions, 2019a).

The five-foot ways are one of the most unique and original activity settings of a Malaysian city (Shamsuddin, 2011). A Malay term 'Kaki Lima' (five-foot way) is one of the major characteristics of Southeast Asian architecture and urban life. It is a covered semi-open space in front of urban houses that allows the pedestrians to walk along a row of shops being shaded from extreme weather conditions, including the sun and heavy downpours. The 'five-foot way' in some ways is reminiscent of a European arcade and can blend the functions of a pedestrian public thoroughfare with a place to display goods and merchandise. The local shop owners used the covered space in front of their premises to display their products, giving the townscape a unique sensory experience through different colours and aromas from various food products, fruits and vegetables (Izumida, 2005; Shamsuddin, 2011). Although associated with Chinese shop-houses, the five-foot ways were used by all members of the community. Today, as a result of diminishing traditional urban fabric, many lots of five-foot ways have disappeared from central KL. The existing five-foot ideas in contemporary KL are more of a tourist attraction than shopping destination for the locals. A traditional 'five-foot way' in KL is shown in Figure 3.1.

Figure 3.1 Five-foot way in old part of central Kuala Lumpur.
Source: M. Kozlowski.

Streets are one of the most crucial element of the urban environment and the primary determinant of its form and function. Streets in cities of Malaysia were always a place of various activities contributing to the vibrancy of the urban centres. The Urban Design Guidelines for KL Central City (DBKL, 2014) identified the following street typologies based on the urban form, character and function: Citywide connector, main shopping streets, character streets, market streets, local connectors, city boulevards, lane and alleys and residential streets. Streets in KLMR are welcoming to members of the community; however, their ethnic preferences very much depend on the type of uses along the streets. Streets with entertainment use such as bars and European style cafes are popular among the Chinese and non-Muslim locals and among the tourists and expats, while market streets and major shopping streets are frequented by all end-users. A good example indicating how different uses can attract various ethnic groups is manifested in the case of the existing three streets in the central part of KL. The streets in question are Jalan Alore, Jalan Arab and Jalan Changkat. All the three streets are within 5-minute walking distance from each other; however, each street is dominated by a different ethnic group. Jalan Alore through its food stalls and outdoor eating specialising in non-halal dishes is popular among Chinese, non-Muslims and tourists. Jalan Arab is a popular destination for Malays and Middle Eastern visitors, while Jalan Changkat lined with bars and night clubs is frequented by expats and Chinese Malaysians. Figure 3.2 (a–i) is a collage of images showing the three streets and three different environments. Other vital streets in central KL include Jalan Tuanku Abdul Rahman, which used to be the main commercial street, and Jalan Petaling, the main shopping street of the city located in the heart of the Chinatown. Jalan Tuanku Abdul Rahman had lost its importance when the main commercial and business activities shifted east to the Bukit Bintang area and KLCC. The street is lined with shops specialising in silk and cotton products and as such attracts mainly Malay and Indian Muslim population. Jalan Petaling has been recently converted to a pedestrian area and is cluttered with stalls and kiosks losing its previous charm and ambience. Petaling Street has become one of the major tourist destinations of the city. The other prominent streets located in the new commercial centre include Jalan Bukit Bintang and part of Jalan Sultan Ismail called 'Bintang Walk' and Jalan Ampang. Bukit Bintang and Bintang Walk are lined with brand shops and multinational food chains, wine bistros and cafes, all portraying a globalised world and as such luring the more affluent clientele deriving from all ethnic groups. Jalan Ampang is one of few urban boulevards in KL lined with tall

Figure 3.2 (a–i) The three streets and three different environments (a–c) Jalan Alore (above) (d–f), Jalan Changkat (centre) and (g–i) Jalan Arab (lower).
Source: M. Kozlowski.

canopy trees (Seng Fatt, 2004). In residential neighbourhoods, there is a strong tradition among the local Malay population to close of streets for social and religious gatherings and festivities such as weddings.

One of the most dominant activities setting in Malaysian cities is markets. Markets can be in the form of open outdoor markets operating throughout the day and in the form of sheltered structure, or a combination of both. The market activities start early in the morning and usually finish mid-afternoon. Markets act as a magnet in attracting crowds of people due to fresh food and a diversity of activities. They also serve as places of social interaction. Although markets are inclusive to all races and ethnic groups, observations of selected markets in the KL region reveal that the Malays are the dominant group (Shamsuddin, 2011). Main indoor markets in central KL include the Chow Kit Market and the Pudu Market. There are a lot of

Figure 3.3 Vacant lot converted to bazar Ramadan in Putrajaya.
Source: M. Kozlowski.

markets operating temporarily. For example, during the Holy Month of Ramadan, vacant lots and streets are converted to markets selling food. Figure 3.3 shows a vacant lot in Putrajaya converted to a Ramadan market. Ramadan markets are frequented solely by Malay and Indian Muslim population.

Shopping centres are semi-private spaces that in the last decades have conquered the minds and souls of all Malaysians. This is visible in the KLMR where the biggest shopping complexes such as Bandar Utama in Damansara, Mid Valley Megamall and Garden Mall complex in KL, Sunway Pyramid in Subang Jaya and IOI in Puchong/Putrajaya are integrated with a diversity of recreational, leisure and entertainment activities and becoming the most popular social interaction places (Shamsuddin, 2011). There are a few exclusive up-market shopping complexes such as the Pavilion, Publica and Star Hill in KL that draw in the affluent clientele from all the three ethnic groups.

According to Shamsuddin (2011), transportation hubs are one of the most dominant activity nodes in major Malaysian cities. In the KLMR, the biggest transportation hubs include NU Sentral and the KLIA. NU Sentral is the first transit-oriented development (TOD) in KLMR comprising four major public transport modes (MRT, LRT, Monorail and commuter train), a large megamall, office towers and international hotels (NU Sentral, 2019).

Towards stronger social cohesion

There are diverse forces in KL working towards stronger social cohesion and inclusion. Two central are the government and the private economic sector. It is worth to mention that the private sector supports events and actions that actively aim to promote social cohesion and to celebrate ethnic diversity. Discussing governmental policy, one must not ignore the dramatic change of 2018 when opposition for the first time in the history of independent Malaysia won the election. The policy before 2018 could be described as a carefully maintained difference—official propaganda (1Malaysia) has been balanced by legal mechanisms supporting the Bumiputera and in effect sidelining the Chinese and Indian populations. The election in 2018 has been won on a promise of fairness and the mobilisation came from all ethnics groups. The first decisions of the government seem to suggest a more inclusive policy, but it has to be seen in hopes of a state for all Malaysians would be fulfilled. The other force acting towards stronger social cohesion is—predominantly Chinese own—private business sector. There are many examples of support of cultural events aiming to strengthen cross-ethnic integration given by private companies. It is relatively easy to understand this approach. First of all, Chinese as a minority (but economically strong) are more vulnerable to any nationalist and populist policies; secondly, the nature of consumer capitalism leads into expanding the consumer base for products and services. In that context, nobody should be surprised that the most diverse urban spaces in KL are shopping centres. These commercial centres, including Suria KLCC, Pavilion, Publica, Bandar Utama, Sunway Pyramid, Mid Valley and IOI, connected by public transport (by roads and railways) create an essential skeleton of the spatial infrastructure of inclusivity in KL.

Major findings

The national unity of all Malaysians is probably still mostly a noble intention and state-sponsored propaganda. There are, however, mechanisms supporting more inclusive (across ethnic and religious barriers) society; some of them are spatial—like public transport and most commercial activities, primarily shopping centres. However, the main structure of KL is profoundly fragmented, and it is almost impossible to imagine what kind of mega-urban projects could lead to stronger spatial and social integration.

A cursory review of major public space types in KLMR in terms of their end-users revealed that there is no imposed urban segregation.

However, public spaces located close to the government and administrative centres or in the proximity of Malay Reserve Lands or large Mosques are dominated by Malays. The Chinese and other non-Muslims may feel a psychological barrier while entering these areas. The ethnic preferences are primarily determined by the type of uses. For example, areas featuring night activities, such as nightclubs and drink bars, are frequented by the non-Muslim Indians, Chinese and Western expats.

There is obviously a need to create spaces that could attract all the ethnic groups. The potential alternative approach may be built out of the experiences of the Kuala Lumpur Bicycle Map, or from the renovation projects that have been undertaken by Think City (the latter will be discussed in Chapter 4). These renovations consist of a bottom-up process of hacking and adjusting urban spaces and have created an environment beyond its designed purposes. This book does not dismiss the inclusive power of big infrastructure projects but would like to stress the importance of more tactical, local and site-specific approach.

Bibliography

Amir, H. A., and Soha, S. (2019) Determinants of a Successful Public Open Space: The Case of Dataran Merdeka in the City Centre of Kuala Lumpur, Malaysia. *Landscape Research*, 44(2), 162–173, DOI:10.1080/01426397.2018.1427221

Anderson, A. H. (2004) *An Introduction to Pentecostalism.* Cambridge: Cambridge University Press.

Butler, G., and Hannam, K. (2014) Performing Expatriate Mobilities in Kuala Lumpur. *Mobilities*, 9(1), 1–20, DOI:10.1080/17450101.2013.784530

Bunnell, T. (2014) The Imports and Travels of Urban Malaysia. In: S. Lemiere, ed. *Misplaced Democracy: Malaysian Politics and People.* Puchong, Selangor: Vinlin Press Sdn Bhd, pp. 91–109.

City Population Putrajaya (2019) www.citypopulation.de/php/malaysia-admin.php?adm1id=16

Department of Statistics, Malaysia (2019) Population Distribution and Basic Demographic Characteristic Report (2019). www.dosm.gov.my/v1/index.php?r=column/ctheme&menu_id=L0pheU43NWJwRWVSZklWdzQ4TlhUUT09&bul_id=MDMxdHZjWTk1SjFzTzNkRXYzcVZjdz09

Dewan Bandaraya Kuala Lumpur (2014) Urban Design Guidelines for Kuala Lumpur City Centre.

Goh, B. L., and Liauw, D. (2009) Post-colonial Projects of a National Culture. *City*, 13(1), 71–79, DOI:10.1080/13604810902726210

Freston, P. (1998) Pentecostalism in Latin America: Characteristics and Controversies. *Social Compass* 45(3), 335–358.

Freston, P. (2004) Contours of Latin American Pentecostalism. In: D.M. Lewis, ed. *Christianity Reborn: The Global Expansion of Evangelicalism in the Twentieth Century.* Grand Rapids, MI and Cambridge: William B. Eerdmans, pp. 221–270.

Fujita, M. A. (2010) Forays into Building Identity. *Journal of Architectural Education,* 63(2), 8–24, DOI:10.1111/j.1531-314X.2010.01055.x

Isa, M., and Kaur, M. (2015) *Kuala Lumpur: Street Names, Guide to their Meaning and Histories.* Singapore: Singapore Marshall Cavendish Editions.

Izumida, H. (2005) Kaki Lima or Five Foot Way as Contesting Space between European and Asian Values. The 1st International Conference of Malay Architecture in Jakarta, 2005, Vol. 1, DOI:10.13140/RG.2.1.3657.6721 www. researchgate.net/publication/283796514_Kaki_Lima_or_Five_Foot_Way_as_Contesting_Space_between_European_and_Asian_Values

Kassim, S. J., Nawami, M. N., and Majid Abdul, N. H. (2017) *The Resilience of Tradition: Malay Illusions in Contemporary Architecture.* Penang Malaysia: Areca Books.

Kay, W. (2013) Empirical and Historical Perspectives on the Growth of Pentecostal-Style Churches in Malaysia, Singapore and Hong Kong. *Journal of Beliefs & Values,* 34(1), 14–25, DOI:10.1080/13617672.2013.759340

Kien, L. C. (2005) Concrete/Concentric Nationalism: The Architecture of Independence in Malaysia, 1945–1969 (PhD Thesis). Berkeley, CA: University of California at Berkeley.

Kozlowski, M. (2014) Revisiting Putrajaya. *Architecture Malaysia,* 26(3), 72–75.

Kozlowski, M., and Mohd Yusof, Y. (2017) Urban Revitalisation in the Tropics: Tale of Two Cities (Singapore and Kuala Lumpur). In: S. Huston, ed. *Smart Urban Regenerations: Visions, Institutions and Mechanisms for Real Estate.* London: Routledge, pp. 120–136.

Kuala Lumpur Attractions (2019a) Batu Caves. www.kuala-lumpur.ws/attractions/batu-caves.htm

Kuala Lumpur Attractions (2019b) KL Eco Forest (formerly) Bukit Nanas Forest Reserve. www.kuala-lumpur.ws/magazine/kl-forest-eco-park.htm

Lim, Z. H. (2017) Kopitiam Ekonomi and the Construction of the Malaysia Neoliberal Subject. In: S. G. Yeoh, ed. *Malaysians and Their Identities.* Petaling Jaya: Strategic Information and Research Development Centre, pp. 63–85.

Manan, S. A., David, M. K., Dumanig, F. P., and Naqeebullah, K. (2015) Politics, Economics and Identity: Mapping the Linguistic Landscape of Kuala Lumpur, Malaysia. *International Journal of Multilingualism,* 12(1), 31–50.

Muniandy, P. (2015) Informality and the Politics of Temporariness: Ethnic Migrant Economies in Little Bangladesh and Little Burma in Kuala Lumpur, Malaysia. *International Sociology,* 30(6), 561–578.

NU Sentral (2019) About Us. www.nusentral.com.

Seng Fatt, L. (2004) *Insiders Kuala Lumpur.* Kuala Lumpur: Marshall Cavendish International Pty Ltd.

Shamsuddin, S. (2011) *Townscape Revisited: Unravelling the Character of the Historic Townscape in Malaysia*. Kuala Lumpur: University Technology of Malaysia UTM Press.

Sheik Ismail, S. N., Sauti, N. S., and Harun, H. N. (2016) Development of Malay Reserve Land: A Case Study of Kuantan. www.pmm.edu.my/zxc/pustaka/writing/data2016/Development%20of%20Malay%20Reserve%20Land.pdf

Sia, K. M., Chin Yew,V., and Siew, C. L. (2018) Influence of FengShui Factors on House Buying Intention of Malaysian Chinese. *Architectural Engineering and Design Management*, 14(6), 427–439, DOI:10.1080/17452007.2018.1466684

South China Morning Post (2017) The Day My Chinese Dad Was Declared a 'Bona Fide' Indonesian and Given a New Name. www.scmp.com/culture/article/2122407/day-my-chinese-dad-was-declared-bona-fide-indonesian-and-given-new-name

Stephens, Q., Kozlowski, M., and Ujang, N. (2016) Contrasting Global Imagery to Local Realities in Postcolonial Waterfronts of Malaysian's Capital Cities. *International Journal of Architecture Research: ArchNet-IJAR*, 10(1), 240–256.

The Guardian (2015) The Bicycle Map Project. www.theguardian.com/cities/2015/sep/18/how-crowd-sourced-map-kuala-lumpurs-ideas-cycling

Ujang, N. (2012) Place Attachment and Continuity of Urban Place Identity. *Procedia-Social and Behavioral Sciences*, 49, 156–167.

Wade, G. (2014) The Origins and Evolution of Ethnocracy. In: S. Lemiere, ed. *Misplaced Democracy: Malaysian Politics and People*. Puchong, Selangor: Vinlin Press SdnBhd, pp. 3–27.

Wan, R., Wan, Omar., Patterson, I., and Pegg, S. (2013) Using a Health Belief Model to Investigate the Walking Behaviour of Residents Living in Kuala Lumpur, Malaysia. *Annals of Leisure Research*, 16(1), 16–38, DOI:10.1080/11745398.2013.769422

World Population Review (2019) Kuala Lumpur Population 2018. http://worldpopulationreview.com/world-cities/kuala-lumpur-population/

Yat-Ming, L. (2012) 'No Chinatown, Please!': Contesting Race, Identity and Postcolonial Memory in Kuala Lumpur. *The Journal of Architecture*, 17(6), 847–870, DOI:10.1080/13602365.2012.746025

Yat Ming, L. (2016) *Architecture and Urban Form in Kuala Lumpur: Race and Chinese Spaces in a Postcolonial City*, 1st ed. Abingdon: Routledge.

4 The spatial dynamics of Kuala Lumpur

Introduction

An inclusive city should be planned and designed to support the physical, economic, cultural and social needs of all people. An inclusive city policy framework targets economic development that creates opportunities for everybody, promotes safe and healthy neighbourhoods for all community groups, provides full access to education, introduces interconnected public transport systems, safeguards and protects natural habitats, creates public spaces for social interaction and ensures the development of usable community facilities (Goltsman and Icafano, 2014).

In the past few decades, Kuala Lumpur and its surrounding metropolitan region have experienced a rapid transformation of its urban form and structure. The chapter seeks to examine how the rapid urban changes have influenced the inclusive character of Kuala Lumpur, which was one of the main attributes of the city since its foundation in the mid-19th century.

The other of this chapter is to identify changes in the spatial structure and urban form of the Kuala Lumpur since the founding of the city in 1857. Although the analysis focuses mainly on the Mahathir and post-Mahathir era from 1981 until the present, the establishment and beginnings of Kuala Lumpur as an urban settlement are also discussed. This chapter also reveals the current trends and looks into the possible scenarios after the May 2018 elections.

The chapter commences with a brief description of the evolution of Kuala Lumpur from a tin mining settlement to one of the major cities of the Malayan Federation. The regional expansion after independence and development of satellite cities are followed by the description of iconic developments and infrastructure projects during the Mahathir era. The conversion of Kuala Lumpur from an inclusive urban environment, accessible to all social groups, to a mega-city dotted with islands containing exclusive gated communities and secluded residential complexes is one of the major emphasis of this chapter. The latest transformations and the path to achieving a global city status are also discussed.

The evolution from tin mining settlement

The first settlement of Kuala Lumpur as a trading post for tin was established by Raja Abdullah in 1857 at the confluence of the Klang and Gombak Rivers. The word 'kuala lumpur' in Malay means the muddy river confluence. In the early stages of urban development, the Gombak and Klang rivers served as an essential transportation route. The first settlers were predominantly Chinese and Indian migrants who came to work in the tin mining industry. The early settlement of Kuala Lumpur resembled a 'cowboy style town' dominated by gambling saloons, bars and brothels (Seng Fatt, 2004; King, 2008; Bunell, 2014).

The Chinese labour migrants had a strong influence on the form and function of early Kuala Lumpur. Yap Ah Loy, The third Kapitan China of the emerging city, was a prominent political figure. As part of his administrative capacity, he played a vital role in the transformation of the tin mining settlement to a new commercial centre (Seng Fatt, 2004).

According to Bunell (2014), Kuala Lumpur was settled and developed mainly by migrant workers whose ancestry can be traced to territories outside cotemporary Malaysia, including China, India, the Arabian Peninsula, Sumatra and Java. The author further asserts that there is a lack of empirical material about the impoverished workers who significantly contributed to building one of Southeast Asia's major urban centres. The history textbooks refer only to the influential men who were part of the management, political and decision-making process.

By the turn of the century, Kuala Lumpur expanded to a medium-sized city. The British colonial powers contributed to the growing urban landscape by developing significant institutional buildings, including the Kuala Lumpur Railway Station and the Sultan Abdul Samad Building. Both buildings are shown as case examples of the British Raja architectural style, which was a combination of Mogul, Moorish and European neo-gothic styles. Reflecting the oriental fantasies of the British colonial powers, both buildings are among the most celebrated landmarks of Kuala Lumpur until today (Bunell, 2014).

At the turn of the century, the city had a few distinctive urban areas, including the British Institutional precinct, the Chinatown with Petaling Street as the primary activity node, the Malay settlement around Masjid Jamek (the Jamek Mosque) and the Indian precinct around Masjid India (The Indian Mosque). Taman Tasik Perdana (Perdana Lake Gardens), the green recreational area, was established at the western fringe of the city in 1888. The area south to the city, designated by Yap Ah Loy, the first China Captain of Kuala Lumpur, for the purpose of the brick production industry was transformed into another pioneer settlement of Kuala Lumpur called Brickfields (Seng Fatt, 2004). The Kuala Lumpur Sanitary Board was established in 1890, and as a result, the first building construction regulations were imposed. The responsibilities of the Board included street maintenance, provision of street lighting and night soil services. The land was divided into building plots, and sanitary lanes were provided at the back of the buildings. Hazardous uses such as abattoirs and brick kilns were relocated away from the town centre (Gullick, 2007).

In the 20th century, the urban areas started to expand away from the rivers' confluence to the north, east and south, witnessing their decline as the significant movement corridors (Shamsuddin et al., 2013; Isa and Kaur, 2015). In the 1920 and 1930s, the city began its expansion with the rail and road systems gradually taking over the function of the main transport movement corridors. The new road system lacked systematic planning and led to major traffic congestion (Abdul Latip et al., 2009). At the brink of the Second World War, the population of Kuala Lumpur just surpassed 170,000 (Yaakob et al., 2019).

The post-independence period

After gaining independence in 1957, Kuala Lumpur was a city predominantly inhabited by Chinese Malaysians, which had a profound impact on the urban form and structure of the city. The dominant building types along the major streets were the Chinese shop-houses, which were built in rows with uniform facades and a continuous covered five footway in front. The shop was always on the ground floor and the residential area on the upper level (Too, 2007). Other building typologies include European classical style villas, Chinese mansions, Malay style free-standing bungalows, institutional and administrative buildings representing the British Raja style. The 1920s and 1930s witnessed the emergence of the art deco style, while the international modernism made a strong presence after the Second World War (Tajuddin, 2007).

On the eve of independence, the major activity areas in the city included the Selangor Padang (now Merdeka Square) with the Selangor Club and the surrounding administration and institutional buildings, Chinatown with Petailing Street, the Railway Station precinct, the Market Square (now Pasar Medan), Pasar Seni (the Central Market). The city of the 1950s was embedded in a tropical landscape foliage (Seng Fatt, 2004).

The stark contrast showing the city skyline of Kuala Lumpur in the early 1950s and today is shown in Figure 4.1a and b.

The challenge for the new Malaysian government in 1957 was to identify a new sense of place and identity for Kuala Lumpur, resulting in the construction of many public buildings that were a reinterpretation of the modernist movement styles originating in the West (Tajuddin, 2007). The post Second World War period was characterised by strong migration from rural areas to Kuala Lumpur. This phenomenon triggered the introduction of planning and zoning regulations derived from the British planning system that constitutes the legal, statutory planning framework of contemporary Malaysia (Tajuddin, 2007).

Kuala Lumpur emerged as a capital of the newly independent Federation of Malayan States in 1957. The city's population at the marking of independence was 316,000 (Yaakob et al., 2019). The expansion of

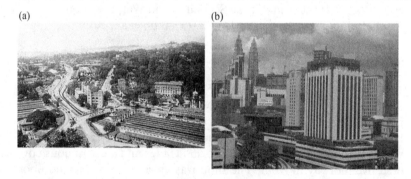

(a)   (b)

Figure 4.1 Skyline of KL in the early 1950s (a, left) and today (b, right).

Sources: www.google.com.my/search?q=view+of+Kuala+Lumpur+in+the+1950s&t bm=isch&source=iu&ictx=1&fir=j0P_bQeGc8IFaM%253A%252CCEdoy PA0VZnEIM%252C_&vet=1&usg=AI4_-kR8YNkMQAZbCdbufCVgMiLpx NtsZQ&sa=X&ved=2ahUKEwig7NXfgtjjAhUQ5o8KHadKCFsQ9QEwB3oECA QQBg#imgrc=j0P_bQeGc8IFaM: and M. Kozlowski.

Note: The image to the left is more than 50 years old and therefore constitutes a public property.

Kuala Lumpur after independence was characterised by the development of planned satellite cities and a significant effort by the federal government to bring Malay population from the rural areas to the city. The city status was granted to Kuala Lumpur in 1972 and this was followed by the establishment of the local authority Dewan Bandaraya Kuala Lumpur (DBKL) (Kuala Lumpur Municipal Council). The appointment by the Federal Government of Malay mayors in a city still predominantly Chinese and Indian was part of the new political agenda (Dewan Bandaraya Kuala Lumpur, 2019).

Since the early 1960s, large parts of the traditional urban fabric featuring traditional Chinese mansions, shop-houses and Malay kampong houses have been demolished to pave the way for new international modernist development. As a result, a substantial portion of Kuala Lumpur's history has been erased. A cursory review of archive images of Kuala Lumpur from the 1920s to 1950s revealed that major streets were lined with deciduous trees providing shade and thermal comfort. Besides, many streets were named after local plants, fruits and animals, which re-emphasises the strong interrelation between the new urban settlement and natural tropical surrounds (Isa and Kaur, 2015). The two Rivers Gombak and Klang, which were the main geographical features and transport routes of the early Kuala Lumpur settlement, have been buried by infrastructure facilities and reduced to two concreted drains (King, 2008). In the early 1960s, Kuala Lumpur was a city with an overwhelming majority of Chinese and Indian Malaysian population. As a result of this demographic imbalance, the new Federal government made efforts to change this proportion and encourage Malay population to settle in Kuala Lumpur. Since the 1960s, the amount of Malay population in Kuala Lumpur and the surrounding new urban centres has significantly increased (Baker, 2008).

One of the major turning points in the development of Kuala Lumpur was the Sino-Malay sectarian riots in May 1969. The riots erupted as a result of the General Elections where the ruling Malay dominated United Malays National Organisation coalition lost a significant amount of seats in favour of the opposition parties controlled mainly by the Chinese and Indians. Despite an increase in the Malay urban population by the end of the 1960s, a majority of the businesses and enterprises in Kuala Lumpur were mainly in the hands of the Chinese Malaysians. The results of the elections created fear among the Malay population of being overwhelmed by the Chinese. As a result of the riots, 196 people were killed, thousands arrested and almost 6,000 homes and businesses destroyed. The Government introduced a state of emergency and suspended Parliament for nearly 2 years. The aftermath of the 1969 riots resulted in the introduction of the New Economic Policy (NEP) with objectives aimed at reducing the economic and wealth gap between the Chinese and the Malays. The NEP had a profound impact on the social and economic environments of Kuala Lumpur, which affected its spatial structure (Baker, 2008; Facts and Details, 2019).

The 1970s witnessed other changes in the visual urban appearance of the city. The retail industry started to witness a gradual makeover. The traditional shop-houses and department stores gradually were replaced by new indoor shopping complexes, which were very much modelled on the western type shopping malls. Ampang Park was the first indoor shopping centre opened in 1973 pioneering the way for future shopping centres in Malaysia and changing shopping habits among the local population. Ampang Park was followed by the development of Wisma Central, which was opened in the late 1970s. Other major shopping centres that opened in the same period include Sungei Wang Plaza and Bukit Bintang Plaza. Private offices located in shop-houses also started to relocate to modern air-conditioned self-contained complexes. (Varghese and Keogh, 2007; Ampang Park Shopping Centre, 2018; Bukit Bintang Plaza, 2018).

The 1960s witnessed the development of first satellite cities, including Shah Alam and Petailing Jaya. Also, new residential townships at the fringe of Kuala Lumpur including Bandar Baru Seri Petailing and Bandar Tun Razak were established (Isa and Kaur, 2015).

The Mahathir Era: the regional expansion

The transformation of the Kuala Lumpur Metropolitan Region (KLMR) since the early 1960s can be labelled as fast-track. Its rapid growth and the development of the satellite edge cities, such as Shah Alam, Petailing Jaya, Subang Jaya, and later Putrajaya and Cyberjaya has been achieved within 50 years as a major goal of the national policy. As a result of this national policy, the city abandoned the regeneration of its traditional heritage style housing and embarked on a model of a sprawled agglomeration with unrestrained motorisation.

In the 1990s and the first decade of the 21st century, the KLMR has witnessed a surge of residential, institutional and commercial development. This development includes large-scale master-planned communities, high-rise residential condominiums and medium-small-scale developments, attached houses and duplex dwellings, large shopping complexes, high-rise office towers, business and technological parks, transportation hubs, university and educational campuses, institutional complexes and international hotels.

In the 1990s, the retail industry started to experience a major revolution. The traditional shopping mall was being replaced by mixed-use megamalls, which apart from retail included other uses such as offices, entertainment and tourist accommodation. One of the most celebrated mixed-use megamalls in Malaysia was Sunway Pyramid opened in 1997. Designed in with an ancient Egyptian theme, Sunway Pyramid contains shops, offices, hotels, entertainment areas, including an indoor ice skating rink and a theme park called Sunway Lagoon. The entire mega-complex was built on the former tin mining fields (Tajuddin, 2012). Other large mega-complexes built in the late 1990s include 1 Utama in Damansara and the Mines Complex in Sri Kebangan.

Although Kuala Lumpur has not yet achieved full World City status like Singapore and Hong Kong, it's been recognised as a 'highly connected gateway city' (Taylor et al., 2002). As a result of global forces, the region has witnessed two major changes. First, the office and up-market housing development, producer services and international service sector are being located in the new Kuala Lumpur City Centre (KLCC).

Second, a semi-urban corridor called Multimedia Super Corridor (MSC) has emerged, including Kuala Lumpur Central City (KLCC), Putrajaya, Cyberjaya and the Kuala Lumpur International Airport (KLIA). Putrajaya became the new administrative capital of Malaysia. In the 1990s, Malaysia's federal government commenced on the development of Putrajaya, located 25 km south of Kuala Lumpur within the new MSC that stretches a further 40 km south to the new KLIA (Rimmer and Dick, 2009; Kozlowski, 2014). The Master Plan for Putrajaya was prepared in the early 1990s by a joint venture of private consultants and government planners. The planning and development control is enforced and coordinated by Putrajaya Corporation (Perbadanan Putrajaya), the local authority managing and administering the development of the city. The Master Plan, a direct response to the overall Structure Plan for the Putrajaya and Sepang areas, was heavily influenced by traditional planning approach promoting the separation of land uses, the designation of a purely administrative/government central precinct surrounded by residential areas with a supporting interlinked web of green spaces. The majorities of residential precincts offer a mix of residential choices ranging from free-standing houses, semi-detached houses, terraced houses and high-rise residential towers. There are small pockets of commercial/retail uses and recreational areas located within each of the precincts (Ho Chin Siong, 2006). According to the King (2008), Putrajaya reflects a utopian image of Pan Malay and Pan Islamic city where the urban environment does not reflect diversified Malaysian urban areas. King further argues that the concept of mixed ethnicity and mixed uses characteristic for the Malaysian urban environment has been neglected in Putrajaya (King, 2008).

The urban structure of the metropolitan region is polycentric and based on a hierarchical distribution of centres connected by a network of transport corridors very similar to a typical model of an American post-industrial city. KLMR contains the primary centre Kuala Lumpur with its Central Business District and Global Command Centre; specialist centres such as Putrajaya, Cyberjaya and KLIA; principal centres such as Shah Alam, Petailing Jaya and Subang Jaya; and several major centres such as Bangi, Serdang, Gombak and Rawang.

In the 1960s and 1970s, public architecture in Malaysia was very much influenced by the modernist style championed by leading international architects, including Le Corbusier and Mies Van Der Rohe. Façade compositions and sun-shading devices were often used to integrate international styles with cultural identity and responsive tropical climate design (Kassim et al., 2017). During the Mahathir era (1981–2003), there was a growing trend among architects in Malaysia to re-install tradition into public buildings, while at the same time incorporating modern functions into the city. The rise of monumental regional architecture in forms of building complexes such as the National Museum (Muzium Negara), the National Theatre (Istana Budaya), Royale Chulan Hotel or even the Kasturi Walk shopping arcade became the new symbols of Malay identity (Kassim et al., 2017).

The anti-western rhetoric of the Mahathir era (1981–2003) resulted in a shift away from the former colonial and Commonwealth connections towards regional Asian knowledge and expertise (Bunell, 2014). Major developments were awarded to Asian companies.

The 1980s witnessed the development of the first high-rise hospitals in Kuala Lumpur and surrounds, which was a deviation from the pre-independence colonial styles featuring climate-responsive low-rise buildings with verandas, large openable windows and high ceilings. Malaysia started to follow the international requirements and criteria for hospital buildings, where the provision of a safe and functional clinical environment was given preference over local climatic conditions and building traditions (Kassim et al., 2017).

The Mahathir era also brought a spate of university campus development in and around Kuala Lumpur where the local architects were trying to resolve the dichotomy between modern western educational requirements and traditional Malay building culture (Kassim et al., 2017).

The 1990s experienced an array of sports facilities development. Many of these facilities, including the National Sports Complex at Bukit Jalal, were built to host the 1998 Commonwealth Games (DBKL, 2012).

The pinnacle of the Mahathir period was the transformation of the Selangor Turf Club, frequented mainly by Chinese, into a World corporate venue and the public area called Kuala Lumpur Central City (KLCC) featuring the twin Petronas Towers. Japanese and South Korean companies played a crucial role in the mega-development. The Twin Towers became not only specific urban landscape artefacts but also a leading selling brand of Malaysia to the rest of the world (Bunell, 2014). The twin Petronas Towers were the tallest building in the world for over a decade. KLCC with the Petronas Towers is shown in Figure 4.2a and b.

(a)   (b)

Figure 4.2 (a and b) KLCC with Petronas Towers—the new landmark of the city and symbol of corporate Malaysia.
Source: M. Kozlowski.

Another visible transformation occurred in the Bukit Bintang area, which was a known sleazy entertainment precinct with the BB Park amusement centre as its star attraction. The Bukit Bintang area featuring night clubs, massage parlors, bars frequented by prostitutes was the pleasure dome for the Chinese residents of Kuala Lumpur. The demolition of BB Park and the development on its site a new shopping mall Sungei Wang Plaza paved the way for a gradual transformation of Bukit Bintang area to an international shopping precinct (Seng Fatt, 2004). Today, Bukit Bintang is the part of the city with the highest concentration of shopping malls in the entire KLMR. However, some entertainment areas in the side streets, including Jalan Alor and Jalan Changkat Bukit Bintang, have been retained.

The firm reference to Malay motifs and traditions in public and commercial architecture, almost excluding the other two other major ethnic groups, is a result of ethnocracy, a systematic political and administrative employment of race-based policies, which originated under the British administration in the 1940s (Wade, 2014). A strong emphasis on the Malay culture can be observed in the urban environment of the new administrative capital of Putrajaya. The early stages of the development of Putrajaya were characterised by Pan Malay and Pan Islamic architectural styles where the new urban environment had nothing in common with the ethnically diversified urban areas of Malaysia (King, 2008). The systematic race base policies favouring one ethnic group have created psychological exclusivity within some urban environments in the KLMR.

An aerial view of central Putrajaya: the main government precinct and Tasik Putrajaya (Putrajaya Lake) is shown in Figure 4.3a and b.

Figure 4.3 Central Putrajaya, the Government Precinct (a, left) and Tasik Putrajaya (Putrajaya Lake) (b, right).
Source: M. Kozlowski.

Towards a global city

The early 21st century witnessed the emergence of a major urban conurbation, including Kuala Lumpur and its surrounding satellite cities. The area of KLMR or Greater Kuala Lumpur is defined as an area covered by ten municipalities surrounding Kuala Lumpur, each governed by the following local authorities: Kuala Lumpur City Hall (DBKL), Putrajaya Municipal Council (Perbadanan Putrajaya), Shah Alam City Council (MBSA), Petaling Jaya City Council (MBPJ), Klang Municipal Council (MPK), Kajang Municipal Council(MPKj), Subang Jaya Municipal Council (MPSJ), Selayang Municipal Council, Ampang Jaya Municipal Council (MPAJ) and Sepang Municipal Council (MPSp). Also, the regional area is spread across two state governments—Selangor and Negri Sembilan—and contains two federal territories. The city of Kuala Lumpur and Putrajaya are designated as Federal Territories under the direct jurisdiction of the Federal Government (International Urban Development Association, 2015).

Contemporary KLMR provides a planned road-based and low-density urban conurbation and in terms of its low density, road-based infrastructure and high car dependency is portrayed as the 'Los Angeles of Southeast Asia' (Rimmer and Dick, 2009). The contemporary Kuala Lumpur Region is marked with a network of highways, modern buildings lacking tropical design features, megamalls and complexes and the traditional Malaysian tropical interaction with a landscape can be traced only along a few streets and within the existing urban kampongs (urban villages) (Kozlowski, 2015).

KLMR is a poly-nuclear megacity although the city of Kuala Lumpur still holds the dominant position as a globalised financial centre. Majority of the ministries have moved to the new administrative capital of Putrajaya; however, that trend was not followed by the diplomatic missions, which still opt for their central Kuala Lumpur location. The leading international gateway to the city of Kuala Lumpur and its metropolitan region is through KLIA, which is located in Sepang 60 km from the centre of Kuala Lumpur.

Sepang is one of the fastest-growing edge cities around the southern fringe of Kuala Lumpur. KLIA opened in 1997 is located in Sepang. Sepang is also home to the Sepang International Circuit featuring the F1 and a part of the MSC. Cyberjaya, Malaysia's first cyber city, established in 1997 on a former palm-oil plantation site is also located within the boundaries of the municipality of Sepang. It is a designated special zone where entrepreneurs and global multinationals enjoy attractive tax breaks, positioning itself to became a global hi-tech destination (Cyberjaya, 2019).

Kajang, one of the oldest settlements in the region, has grown to a substantial city with a population of over 400,000. Other edge cities including Ampang, Subang Jaya and Sungai Buloh have grown to considerable major urban centres.

The first planned township of Petailing Jaya has developed into a major city with a population over 500,000. It is currently a leading urban centre to become a sustainable residential and major commercial centre (Petaling Jaya City Council, 2019).

Since the 1990s, urban development in the KLMR has followed the global trends and has been influenced by the notion of neoliberalism. This resulted in property-led development, which has become one of the main drivers of the national economy. Neoliberalism emerged strongly in the late 1970s in North America and Western Europe in the era of stagnation and economic recession. It has strongly influenced urban policies, especially in large global cities. Instead of preserving and enhancing public spaces and promoting affordable residential precincts, urban local authorities prefer to create semi-privatised and revenue-producing enclaves and promote gentrification to boost the image of the city to the outside world (Purcell, 2011).

The aftermath of the Mahathir period can be characterised by influences of globalisation neoliberalism resulting in fast-track development. The lack of regional physical planning and coordination has led to urban sprawl and degradation of character areas and neighbourhoods.

According to Morshidi and Abdul Rahim (2010), Kuala Lumpur was transformed within a decade (1990–2000) from a sleepy capital to a diversified and thriving international centre. The development of KLCC, KLIA and the MSC, including Putrajaya and Cyberjaya, all contributed to this elevated city status.

As a result, since 2000, there has been a visible sharp increase in property prices with Kuala Lumpur and Selangor declared as areas where houses fall in a 'severely unaffordable category'. The other reason for the sharp rise in prices is the growing demand for housing and also high foreign ownership of the housing stock, which in some parts of central Kuala Lumpur is as high as 20% (Malaysia My Second Home, 2018).

The rapid development of the KLMR together with the large influx of population from other parts of the country and the issue of illegal migrants from overseas has no doubt contributed to the rise of crime (Sidhu, 2005). According to 2017 Crime Index by Numbeo Kuala Lumpur has the highest crime index and lowest safety index among major cities in Southeast Asia. Although the amount of major crimes, including murder and manslaughter, is relatively low, petty crimes such as motorbike and car theft and house brake-ins boost the figures (Numbeo, 2018).

As a result of the rapid growth and safety and security concerns, numerous small- to medium-size gated communities have mushroomed in the metropolitan region, creating a fragmented network of exclusive urban utopias. Development of self-contained townships such as Desa Parkcity and Setia Alam, where secluded residential areas are sealed off and the general public space is limited to shopping malls, and recreational parks only add to the gradual growth of 'fortress Kuala Lumpur'.

Davies (2006) introduced the term 'fortress L.A (Los Angeles)' where he described the rapidly growing private realm of Los Angeles secluded and gated from the rest of the city and the poorer neighbourhoods. A similar phenomenon is happening in KLMR, where the growing concern of living in safe and secure environments contributes to the growth of privatised residential areas, up-market residential complexes and semi-private mixed-use mega malls. As a result of growing 'safety paranoia', even middle-income neighbourhoods are sealing themselves off and engaging security guards for protection.

Former residential neighbourhoods converted to semi-gated communities are shown in Figure 4.4a and b.

In the past decade, urban growth has been intensively encroaching on the existing greenfield areas, and the lack of regional planning policies prevents the local authorities and government departments to reverse this process. This rapid urban sprawl is swallowing up the traditional inner and outer city kampong areas. According to Pacione (2005), the growth of the city into the surrounding rural areas is a

(a)   (b)

Figure 4.4 (a and b) Former residential areas converted to gated communities.
Source: M. Kozlowski.

common phenomenon in Southeast Asia, especially in Malaysia and Indonesia. However, in the KLMR, many of these kampong areas are being pulled down to pave the way for new residential neighbour-hoods. The existing heritage protection legislation does not cover tra-ditional kampong areas and its character architecture, sense of place and identity. Even Kampung Baru, the traditional Malay urban en-clave located in the central part of Kuala Lumpur, was of interest to developers responding to the high plot ratios designated for this area by the local authority. An example of intrusion of new development into traditional Kampung area is shown in Figure 4.5.

The development industry once dominated very strongly by the gov-ernment sector has now been infiltrated by the private sector. Large developers such as YTL, Gamuda Berhad, Setia, Sain Darby and IOI have entered the market and gained considerable influence on the future transformation of Kuala Lumpur and its entire metropolitan region. The property-led development has become one of the main driving forces of the national economy.

The central part of Kuala Lumpur has still retained its distinc-tive urban environments, each featuring activities targeting a specific user group. In Kuala Lumpur, social segregation of space is de-pendent on the types of activities attracting different social groups. In central Kuala Lumpur, there are several such activity precincts including Petaling Street and Chinatown targeting tourist and the Chinese Malaysia Population, Masjid India popular among Muslim Indian and Malays, Kampung Baru frequently visited by Malay

Figure 4.5 Intrusion of new development into a traditional kampong area.
Source: M. Kozlowski.

families from all over the region, Brickfields, the ethnic Indian precinct, and finally entertainment areas along Jalan P. Ramlee and Jalan Changkat Bukit Bintang visited regularly by the expat population. The Bukit Bintang area converted from a 'sleazy' entertainment area to a popular shopping and entertainment area is slowly being transformed into a global shopping destination featuring high-end shopping complexes such as Star Hill and Pavilion. The former popular centre Bukit Bintang Plaza has been demolished and is currently being redeveloped for a more exclusive shopping destination. Its neighbour Sungei Wang Plaza is being refurbished for more up-market complex focusing on brand stores and speciality shops. The affordable shopping enclaves around Bukit Bintang are slowly becoming a thing of the past.

The rapid development in the KLMR has opened discourse on the necessity of imposing tropical and sustainable planning and design requirements on future developments.

Development in KLMR is coordinated through local plans prepared by the different local authorities. There is no regional plan for the entire metropolitan area. In the city of Kuala Lumpur development is controlled and promoted by the Kuala Lumpur 2020 City Plan (a strategic planning document) and the Kuala Lumpur Development Control Plan (a statutory planning document) (DBKL, 2012).

The previous 1984 Kuala Lumpur Structure Plan (KLSP) was aimed at ensuring that sufficient housing would be provided for all income groups in the city and that housing was distributed adequately for all the residents. One of the main objectives of the Plan was to eliminate squatter residential development in the city, which was almost accomplished by 2010.

In contrast, the main priorities of the 2020 City Plan are to create a sustainable and world-class city. In parallel with the decline of the City Centre residential population, there has been a significant drop in residential zone land area from 523 hectares in 1984 to 288 hectares in 2010. The decline in residential land in the City Centre is due to the redevelopment of some of the older housing areas into office, commercial and mixed uses. Land previously zoned residential has been rezoned to commercial or mixed-use. As a result, existing low-density housing areas are occupying the land, which has high potential commercial value. Pressures will remain on these remaining pockets of residential land to redevelop for commercial and mixed-use purposes which, in turn, could lead to a further reduction of residential population in the central city area (DBKL, 2012). Although residential development is permissible in commercial and mixed-use zones, such development is usually associated with high-quality commercial uses situated on the lower levels. Mixed-use development complexes in central city areas often attract high-end property value residential development. Currently, land prices in the city centre vary between 20,000 and 30,000 Malaysian Ringgit per square metre (5,000–7,000 USD). Such high prices eliminate the possibility of developing affordable housing (Malaysia My Second Home, 2018).

As a result of massive fast track development, Kuala Lumpur has experienced environmental degradation with a significant loss of green open space. The green space per capita ratio has decreased from 13.5 m^2 per inhabitant in 2010 to 8 m^2 in 2014 (Abu Kasim et al., 2019). The figure of 8 m^2 of green open space per inhabitant is below the minimum of 9 m^2 recommended by the World Health Organisation and significantly lower than that of neighbouring Singapore where every resident can enjoy 66 m^2 of green open space. The situation in other cities of the metropolitan region is better. For example, 38% of Putrajaya is green open space, although there is not enough residential population to take full advantage of this asset (Kozlowski, 2014).

The Federal Government and DBKL are responding to the loss of green space in Kuala Lumpur and have initiated the creation of new green space (Taman Tugu) close to the central area. Taman Tugu is a welcome addition to KL's green spaces, which are under permanent threat from urban development. The park opened in September 2018 to conserve a 30-hectare green-lung in the middle of Kuala Lumpur and turn it into an urban forest park open to the public (Malaysia Traveller, 2019).

The rapid urban development also had a profound impact on the character and ambience of the urban conurbation. The analysis of the selected streets and public spaces in the KLMR identified a few distinct stereotypes. Firstly, the streets in the remaining older parts of the city retained some form of the sense of place and identity. The on-going street activities, building form and characterfully or partially respond to the local tropical settings. Secondly, there are the transition zones, such as Jalan Pudu, which cater mainly for vehicular and pedestrian movement and where little attention has been given to the local surrounds and climate. Thirdly there are the globalised spaces (Jalan Bukit Bintang) where the physical design is mainly aimed at creating high-end shopping precincts to attract visitors (international and domestic) and business operators. There are also traditional popular outdoor seating areas such as Jalan Alor and Jalan Arab. Tropical design is applied mainly in creating outdoor eating enclaves for international tourists. And finally there the synthetic environments built to portray a particular image to the rest of the world. These specific environments include KLCC and Persiaran Perdana. KLCC, developed as a joint venture of the private and public sectors, portrays an image of a 'modern and corporate Malaysia' while Persurian Perdana in Putrajaya built by the federal government represents a metaphor of a strong legislative, judicial and executive power giving a boost and popularity to the ruling political establishment. KLCC developed an artificial tropical environment as a backdrop for surrounding luxury buildings, and the developers of Persurian Perdana created a sizeable European style boulevard softened by tropical vegetation and flanked by institutional buildings, many of them with a strong resemblance to the Middle Eastern styles (Kozlowski, Ujang and Maulan, 2015).

One of the unique characteristics of urban areas in Southeast Asia mainly in Indonesia and Malaysia is that a significant number of the urban population still live in urban kampungs (urban villages), which are predominantly unplanned and primarily low-income residential areas (Pacione, 2005). The KLMR has a whole network of inner-city and outer city kampungs that are gradually being engulfed by the growing high-density urban areas and slowly disappearing under the hammer of new development.

The Federal Government and the local authority DBKL have high ambitions in radically improving the built environment and transforming Kuala Lumpur into a world-class city. A series of catalyst projects and new policies have been introduced. The three major urban catalyst projects currently under construction that will significantly contribute in transforming the urban environment of the city are the River of Life (ROL) Project, Tun Razak Exchange and the Klang Valley Mass Rapid Transit (MRT).

The two significant developments undergoing currently in central Kuala Lumpur are the River of Life Project and the Tun Razak Exchange. The River of Life (ROL) is a seven-year project headed by the Federal Government of Malaysia to transform the Klang and Gombak Rivers, going through the old centre of Kuala Lumpur, into a vibrant and liveable waterfront with high economic value. The entire project covers eight rivers with total length of 110 km, and is divided into three major components, i.e. River Cleaning (led by the Department of Irrigation & Drainage (DID) Malaysia), River Beautification (led by Kuala Lumpur City Hall (DBKL)) and Commercialisation and Tourism (driven Ministry of Federal Territory (KWP)). Part of the River beautification around Masjid Jamek (the old City Mosque) was completed and opened to the public in 2017. (River of Life, 2019).

Tun Razak Exchange (TRX) is a property development project built on 30-hectare area in the heart of Kuala Lumpur by 1 Malaysia Development Berhad (1MDB). The area was used as quarters for civil servants until late 1990s and as Pasar Rakyat, a marketplace for dried food items and souvenirs. This catalyst project is part of the Economic Transformation Programme aimed to help Malaysia gain a high-income economy in 2020 and to create a vibrant financial district in Kuala Lumpur. The master plan for the TRX focuses on integrated infrastructure development, ensuring high quality of comfort and sustainability to its communities, including comprehensive transportation links alongside international institutions and support services. A central park featuring terraced gardens and water features will connect all the buildings of the new financial district. The first stage of the development is due to be completed by the end of 2019 (Tun Razak Exchange, 2019; TRX My City, 2019).

The completed part of the River of Life Project and Tun Razak Exchange, under development, are shown in Figure 4.6a and b.

(a)   (b)

Figure 4.6 Completed part of the River of Life Project (a, left) and the Tun Razak Exchange –under development (b, right).

Source: M. Kozlowski.

Significant challenges of contemporary Kuala Lumpur and its metropolitan region include the heat island effect, flash flooding and traffic congestion (Morshidi and Abdul Rahim, 2010). To address the traffic congestion, the Federal Government has established a Land Public Transport Agency (SPAD) in 2010 with the responsibility of coordinating and managing the development and operation of land public transport in Malaysia. SPAD took an active role in organizing the further development of public transportation in KLMR by expanding the existing LRT (light rail system) and building a new MRT (Mass Rapid Transit) network serving the entire urban region (SPAD, 2016). As a result of the first transit-oriented developments such as NU Sentral, comprising different transport modes, commercial, retail and office uses were constructed (NU Sentral, 2019).

In the last years, the federal and state governments and local authorities have introduced new initiatives to reverse the destruction of the traditional urban fabric as well as to initiate the design and construction of new climate-responsive tropical built form. The establishment of organisations such as Think City (an NGO sponsored by federal institutions) and Urbanice Malaysia (a federal government subsidiary) to undertake small-scale urban regeneration projects and create better cities is a step forward in mitigating the fast-track property-led development impacts. The Green Building Index (GBI) of Malaysia, introduced in 2009, addresses residential, commercial and institutional development as well as hotels, tourist resorts, townships. GBI aims to promote tropical sustainable design and to reduce negative environmental impacts by improving energy and water efficiency, waste reduction and sustainable management (Shari, 2015).

In the Ninth Malaysian Plan, the National Heritage Act 2005 was enacted to give protection and preserve the cultural heritage and unique natural habitats. The Act addresses conservation and preservation of natural heritage, tangible and intangible, cultural heritage, and underwater cultural heritage (Ghafar, 2010). A major achievement in historic conservation took place in 2009 by placing Old Georgetown and Old Town Melaka on the World UNESCO Heritage list. Nevertheless, the National Heritage Act has not been that successful in practice. Currently, in Central Kuala Lumpur several listed historic buildings remain empty and underutilised and as such plunging into further deterioration. For example, two famous historic buildings, the former Loke Chow Kit Department Store (now partially occupied by the industrial court) and the former Town Hall and Sanitary Board, are largely unoccupied and disused.

Kuala Lumpur forty years and today

Kuala Lumpur has been undergoing massive transformation since independence, which has only accelerated during the 1980s. A survey conducted by Somasundram Sambasivan, Rasiah and Pei Leng (2018) revealed that there is a mismatch between urban policy measures and outcomes desired by the urban community of Kuala Lumpur. The urban community is not given sufficient opportunities to voice their opinions and providing input in designing policies on urban liveability. According to Watson (2011), current urban planning often neglects the livelihoods of the urban poor and serves the urban elite interests, resulting in socially and spatially exclusive neighbourhoods. An interview with a Non-Government Organisation, Coalition to Save Kuala Lumpur (CSKL), revealed that large section of the residential community feel that basic social needs such as quality public areas and amenities, affordable public housing and providing good urban infrastructure have been neglected and sidelined and overshadowed by high-end international development projects.[1]

Regarding the KLMR, the primary question remains: have all the transformations and dynamic spatial changes in past decades had a positive impact on the urban environment? Are the end-users, including residents, local business operators and visitors (employees, shoppers, etc.), satisfied with the transformation? To answer these questions, it is imperative to seek the opinions and subjective views of people who remember Kuala Lumpur 40 years ago before the fast track development took a rapid pace.

The information on the subjective views of local residents and visitors to Kuala Lumpur 40 years ago and today is obtained through conducting a close-ended questionnaire. The purpose of this survey is to gain information about people's perception of the urban environment of Kuala Lumpur 40 years ago and today. This questionnaire addresses issues including visual quality, urban form and structure, functioning, safety and maintenance. A sample of 50 respondents representing the three major ethnic groups is selected for this exercise. Each individual respondent has to be 50 years and above.

The questionnaire survey revealed a powerful nostalgia among representatives of all three ethnic groups to the Kuala Lumpur's environment of the 1980s. A majority of respondents noted that the 'old Kuala Lumpur' had more character, sense of place and identity. The city in the 1980s was more climate-responsive and had a robust tropical ambience. The traffic jams were not as intensive as today, and the principal streets were lined with canopy trees providing shade and thermal comfort. According to a majority of respondents, the city of the 1980s had a better sense of orientation than the city today. The built environment in 1980 comprised of a significant amount of traditional building, which contributed to creating a sense of place and identity. Almost all respondents indicated that the city was much safer than today.

The questionnaire form is included in Appendix 4.1.

Post-2018 elections

The new Pakatan Harapan Government that unexpectedly won the general elections in May 2018 ending the 61-year continuous rule of the Barisan National political establishment has not yet identified its urban policy. However, concerned with the rising national debt they have commenced with placing major public transport projects on hold. These projects included the proposed High-Speed Rail to Johor Bahru, Iskandar Putra and Singapore, the MRT3 planned as a circle line for the KLMR. The third major public project shelved was the East Coast Rail Link (ECRL) between Kuala Lumpur and Kuantan (The Star, 2018).

For the first year in power the new government was mainly focusing on exemplifying mistakes and errors of the previous administration. There was a lot of rhetoric on introducing local elections and increasing community participation, but as yet no measures and actions have been taken. Mayors are still appointed by the federal and state governments. Initiatives such as the street pedestrian upgrades in Masjid India and Chinatown promoted by the Federal Territories Ministry and DBKL, or the sustainable retrofitting of existing government buildings championed by the Ministry of Energy, Science, Technology, Environment and Climate Change, are just cosmetic changes (The Edge Financial Daily, 2019; The Star, 2019a).

However, in the second half of 2019 there was a shift in the approach. The government announced that it is committed to delivering the much-needed Rapid Transit System (RTS) between Johor Bharu and Singapore. The project, due to be completed by 2024, will benefit the emerging Iskandar Region in Johor and trigger a possible future rapid transport connection between Johor and Kuala Lumpur (The Star, 2019). In October 2019 the government gave a green light to proceed with the East Coast Rail Link between Kuala Lumpur and Kuantan (The Star, 2019).

Lately, the DBKL has initiated a new community-oriented Kuala Lumpur 2040 Development Plan. With the drafting of the plan DBKL is now focused on a strategic plan that incorporates community values and one that sets out a more sustainable vision of the city's future.

To achieve this, the draft Kuala Lumpur Structure Plan 2040 (KLSP2040) and Kuala Lumpur Local Plan 2040 (KLLP2040) will be in tandem with national aspirations, vision and the sustainable development goals. The Plan will introduce new concepts in planning and development, and address issues such as the housing for the elderly, micro-housing as well as urban and vertical green infrastructures (The Star, 2019).

However, the new administration has not yet established a vision for the entire KLMR and the improvement of its public realm. No attempts have been made to repeal the orthodox planning legislation and introduce sustainable planning and design as the backbone for any new development.

Major findings

The development and transformation of Kuala Lumpur and its surrounding region since the Second World War had a similar pattern to the growth of other major capitals of Southeast Asia including Bangkok, Ho Chi Minh City, Jakarta and Manilla. All these cities have expanded into major urban conurbations where physical development has been given preference over any urban community agendas. The exception to this rule was Singapore, where the top-down approach and central controlled physical planning monitored and coordinated development since the early 1970s.

However, the transformation of Kuala Lumpur and its surrounding metropolitan region has been more extraordinary in comparison with the other major cities of Southeast Asia as the KLMR is not a territory in its own right but an integral part managed by the federal and two state governments. Also, KLMR comprises ten different local authorities, each with different objectives and planning agendas. Since the 1980s, the development controls, land use regulations and planning strategies were often overridden by development priorities that moved the city forward on the trajectory of achieving global economic status. Until now, there has been no attempt to create a regional strategy and a regional body incorporating representatives from all ten local authorities, the federal and state governments.

Based on the literature review and document search Kuala Lumpur was recognised as an inclusive city until the mid-1980s. The public spaces and community facilities were accessible to all members of the community, and the feeling of safety was reasonably high. There is no doubt that the current transformations have improved the city's international competitiveness standing and opened a door for multi-national companies and foreign investment. However, findings derived from the questionnaire survey, structured interviews and other relevant community studies reveal a growing gap between community expectations and current urban policies. There is an increasing community dissatisfaction and feeling that the city is losing its character and ambience, and it's progressing towards a more unsafe urban environment.

Nevertheless, there are some achievements on behalf of the federal government and the local authorities. The public transport is the best in Southeast Asia after Singapore and operates on a regional scale covering distant areas of the urban conurbation. Although the region is experiencing adverse impacts of climate change such as frequent and severe thunderstorms' and the 'urban heat island effect', its overall impact is lesser than in other capital of Southeast Asia including Jakarta and Bangkok.

The KLMR is continually expanding without any signs of stopping. It's still waiting for a proper vision that would sustain the existing uncontrolled growth and reintroduce community-oriented projects adding some local tropical character that has been lost in the last decades.

Note

1 Based on interview with representative of Coalition to Save Kuala Lumpur (CSKL) carried out in April 2019.

Bibliography

Abdul Latip, N. S., Heath, T., and Liew, M. S. (2009) A Morphological Analysis of the Waterfront in City Centre, Kuala Lumpur. INTA-SEGA Bridging Innovation, Technology and Tradition Conference Proceedings. Grand Mercure Fortune, 2–4 December 2009.

Abu Kassim, J., Mohd Yusof, J., and Mohd Shafri, Z. (2019) Urban Space Degradation: An Experience of Kuala Lumpur City. *Environmental Management and Sustainable Development*, 1(1), 27–41.

Ampang Park Shopping Centre (2018) www.ampangpark.com.my/#3

Baker, J. (2008) *Crossroads: A Popular History of Malaysia and Singapore.* Singapore: Marshall Cavendish.

Bukit Bintang Plaza (2018) www.kuala-lumpur.ws/klareas/bukitbintang_shopping.htm

Bunnell, T. (2014) The Imports and Travels of Urban Malaysia. In: S. Lemiere, ed. *Misplaced Democracy: Malaysian Politics and People.* Puchong, Selangor: Vinlin Press Sdn Bhd, pp. 91–109.

Cyberjaya (2019) History of Cyberjaya. www.cyberjayamalaysia.com.my/

Davies, M. (2006) *City of Quartz: Excavating the Future in Los Angeles.* London and New York: Verso Publication.

Dewan Bandaraya Kuala Lumpur (DBKL) (Kuala Lumpur City Hall) (2012) Kuala Lumpur City Plan 2020.

Dewan Bandaraya Kuala Lumpur (2019) DBKL History. www.dbkl.gov. my/index.php?option=com_content&view=article&id=39&Itemid=174& lang=en

Facts and Details (2019) Racial Discord in Malaysia. http://factsanddetails.com/southeast-asia/Malaysia/sub5_4a/entry-3625.html#targetText=There%20were%20bloody%20race%20riots,least%20200%20people%20were%20killed

Ghafar., A. (2010) *Heritage Interpretations of the Built Environment: Experiences from Malaysia.* http://www.heritage.gov.hk/conference2011/en/pdf/7_Prof%20Ghafar%20Ahmad.pdf

Goltsman, S., and Icafano, D. (2014) Design Case: The Inclusive City: Designing Cities that Meet The Human Needs. Paper presented at UD International Conference, Lund, Sweden, June 2014. http://ud2014.se/presentations/the-inclusive-city-designing-cities-that-meet-human-needs/

Gullick, J. M. (2007) The Early Kuala Lumpur. In: Chow Von Fee, ed. *The Encyclopedia of Malaysia: Architecture.* Singapore and Kuala Lumpur: Archipelago Press, pp. 74–76.

Ho Chin Siong (2006) Putrajaya – Administrative Capital of Malaysia: Planning Concept and Implementation. Paper delivered at the Sustainable Urban Development and Governance Conference in Sung Kyun Kwan University, Seoul, South Korea.

International Urban Development Association (INTA) (2015) Kuala Lumpur Metropolitan Malaysia. https://inta-aivn.org/en/481-inta/activitities/exchange/roundtables/20122013-inbetween/1769-kuala-lumpur-metropolitan

Isa, M., and Kaur, M. (2015) *Kuala Lumpur: Street Names, Guide to their Meaning and Histories.* Singapore: Singapore Marshall Cavendish Editions.

Kassim, S. J., Nawami, M. N., and Majid Abdul, N. H. (2017) *The Resilience of Tradition: Malay Illusions in Contemporary Architecture.* Penang Malaysia: Areca Books.

King, R. (2008) *Kuala Lumpur and Putrajaya: Negotiating Urban Space in Malaysia.* Singapore: NUS Press.

Kozlowski, M. (2014) Revisiting Putrajaya. *Architecture Malaysia*, 26(3), 72–75.

Kozlowski, M. (2015) Kuala Lumpur: Transformation towards a World City Built Environment. *Architecture Malaysia*, 27(2), 70–75.

Kozlowski, M., Ujang, N., and Maulan, S. (2015) Performance of Public Spaces in Kuala Lumpur Metropolitan Region in Terms of Tropical Climate. *Alam Cipta* (Special Issue 1 December 2015), 41–51.

Malaysia My Second Home (2018) A Closer Look at the Greater Kuala Lumpur Property Market. www.mm2h.com/a-closer-look-at-the-greater-kuala-lumpur-property-market/

Malaysia Traveller (2019) Taman Tugu Forest Trail. www.malaysia-traveller.com/taman-tugu-forest-trail.html

Morshidi, S., and Abdul Rahim, A. (2010) Going Global: Development, Risks and Responses in Kuala Lumpur and Putrajaya. In: S. Hamnet and D. Forbes, eds. *Planning Asian Cities: Risks and Resilience.* London and New York: Routledge. pp. 220–240.

Numbeo (2018) Crime Index 2017. www.numbeo.com/crime/

NU Sentral (2019) About Us. www.nusentral.com.

Pacione, M. (2005) *Urban Geography: A Global Perspective.* New York: Routledge.

Petailing Jaya City Council (2019) City Background. www.mbpj.gov.my/en

Purcell, M. (2011) Neoliberalisation and Democracy in: Readings. In: S. Fainstein and S. Campbell, eds. *Urban Theory.* London: John Wiley and Sons, pp. 42–55.

Rimmer, P. J., and Dick, H. (2009) *The City in Southeast Asia: Patterns, Processes and Policy.* Singapore: NIUS Press.

River of Life (2019) About River of Life. www.klriver.org/

Seng Fatt, L. (2004) *Insiders Kuala Lumpur.* Kuala Lumpur: Marshall Cavendish International Pty Ltd.

Shamsuddin, S., Abdul Latip, N., and Ulaiman, A. B (2013) *Regeneration of the Historic Waterfront: An Urban Design Compendium for Malaysian Waterfront Cities.* Kuala Lumpur: ITBM.

Shari, Z. (2015) Greening Tourism in Malaysia. *FutureArc: The Voice of Green Architecture in Asia-Pacific,* 41, 122–123.

Sidhu, A. S. (2005) The Rise of Crime in Malaysia: An Academic and Statistical Analysis. *Journal of the Kuala Lumpur Royal Malaysia Police College,* 4, 1–28. http://rmpckl.rmp.gov.my/Journal/BI/riseofcrime.pdf

Somasundram, S., Sambasivan, M., Rasiah, R., and Pei Leng, T. (October 2018) Ranking the Challenges of the Urban Community in Malaysia. *Institution and Economics,* 10(4), 69–89.

SPAD (2016) Land Public Transport Transformation in Malaysia – History, Aspirations and Challenges. www.spad.gov.my/sites/default/files/chairman_speech-22april20161.pdf

Tajuddin, M. (2007a) Developing a Modern Malaysian Architecture. In: Chow Von Fee, ed. *The Encyclopedia of Malaysia: Architecture.* Singapore and Kuala Lumpur: Archipelago Press, pp. 106–108.

Tajuddin, M. (2007b) The Rise of Modernism. In: Chow Von Fee, ed. *The Encyclopedia of Malaysia: Architecture.* Singapore and Kuala Lumpur: Archipelago Press, pp. 98–99.

Tajuddin, M. (2012) *Architecture, Society and Nation Building: Multiculturalism, Democracy and Islam.* Johor Bharu: Pustaka Global Resources.

Taylor, P. J, Walker, D., Catalano, G., and Hoyler, M. (2002) Diversity and Power in the World City Network. *Cities*, 19(4), 231–241.

The Edge Financial Daily (2019) Cenergi SEA Eyes Government Lighting Retrofit Project. www.theedgemarkets.com/article/cenergi-sea-eyes-government-lighting-retrofit-project

The Star (2018) Government Scraps MRT 3 Project. www.thestar.com.my/news/nation/2018/05/31/govt-scraps-mrt-3-project-pm-we-must-reduce-our-borrowings/

The Star (2019a) Khalid: Decision on Jalan TAR 'pedestrian walk' by March 15. www.thestar.com.my/~/media/online/2019/02/19/15/01/khalidsamad.ashx/?w=620&h=413&crop=1&hash=6DB916E82CFFC05923524F6150BBB0BEAE5527B3

The Star (2019b) Malaysia's China-Backed US$10.5 Billion East Coast Rail Link Back on Track, Foreign Minister Says. www.thestar.com.my/news/regional/2019/09/12/malaysias-china-backed-us105-billion-east-coast-rail-link-back-on-track-foreign-minister-says

The Star (2019c) MCA: Resume Johor-Singapore RTS Project. www.thestar.com.my/news/nation/2019/10/19/mca-resume-johor-singapore-rts-project

The Star (2019d) People-Centric Plan for KL. www.thestar.com.my/metro/metro-news/2019/10/29/people-centric-plan-for-kl?fbclid=IwAR0IsC36fspomKeq2U_Nn_4BQSd-VH5XpiRHJZ6WPpZ3gGCXXN7QlbTs-tg

Too, A. (2007) The Chinese Shop-House. In: Chow Von Fee, ed. *The Encyclopedia of Malaysia: Architecture*. Singapore and Kuala Lumpur: Archipelago Press, pp. 90–92.

TRX My City (2019) Tun Razak Exchange Over the Years. https://trx.my/city/tun-razak-exchange-over-the-years

Tun Razak Exchange (2019) TRX Malaysia – A New World Class Financial District. www.tunrazakexchange.com/tun-razak-exchange-tax-incentives/

Varghese, J., and Keogh, S. (2007) Industrial and Commercial Architecture. In: Chow Von Fee, ed. *The Encyclopedia of Malaysia: Architecture*. Singapore and Kuala Lumpur: Archipelago Press, pp. 118–120.

Wade, G. (2014) The Origins and Evolution of Ethnocracy. In: Chow Von Fee, ed. *Misplaced Democracy: Malaysian Politics and People*. Puchong, Selangor: Vinlin Press Sdn Bhd, pp. 3–27.

Watson, V. (2011) Inclusive Urban Planning for the Working Poor: Planning Education Trends and Potential Shift. Women in Informal Employment, Globalizing and Organizing (WIEGO) Working Paper (Urban Policies) No. 21.

Yaakob, U., Masron, T., and Masami, F (2019) Ninety Years of Urbanization in Malaysia: A Geographical Investigation of Its Trends and Characteristics. www.ritsumei.ac.jp/acd/re/krsc/hss/book/pdf/vol04_05.pdf#targetText=Consequently%2C%20Kuala%20Lumpurs%20population%20reached,status%20of%20a%20Federal%20Territory

APPENDIX 1: Questionnaire Survey-Kuala Lumpur 40 years ago and today

Question	Answer 1	Answer 2	Answer 3
1 What were the commercial, institutional, and residential buildings in Kuala Lumpur like 40 years ago	More traditional and responding to the tropical climate and local conditions	More or less similar to the building appearance today	More chaotic and devoid of traditional features
2 What was the condition of the streets in Kuala Lumpur 40 years ago	Major streets were lined with canopy trees which provided a lot of shade, reduced the air temperature and created comfort for the passing by pedestrians	More or less similar to the streets today	Streets were devoid of trees exposed to the sun and not well maintained
3 What were the basic characteristics of public spaces (squares and small plazas) in Kuala Lumpur 40 years ago	The public spaces provided a good sense of identity and belonging	Their characteristic were similar to the public spaces we have today	The public spaces 40 years ago did not represent any specific character or sense of belonging
4 What was the sense of orientation and navigation in Kuala Lumpur 40 years ago	The city was more compact and as such it was easy to navigate and find your way. The sense of orientation was good	More or less similar condition to what we have today	More disorganised with worse sense of orientation than the city today
5 What was the condition of public parks in Kuala Lumpur 40 years ago	The public parks were well maintained in good condition and frequented by people	More or less in similar condition to what we have today	The parks were not well maintained and as such less popular among people than parks today

(*Continued*)

Question	Answer 1	Answer 2	Answer 3
6 How can you describe the general character of Kuala Lumpur 40 years ago	It was a city with many traditional buildings (e.g., shop-houses, colonial buildings, bungalows), traditional shops and markets. There were a lot of trees along the streets	More or less similar character to the city today	It did not have any character—no defined or specific feature
7 In terms of aesthetic values- what was the urban environment of Kuala Lumpur 40 years ago	Aesthetically more pleasing than today	More or less the same as the urban environment today	Aesthetically less pleasing- than the urban environment today
8 What was the condition of the pedestrian environment of Kuala Lumpur 40 years ago	The sidewalks were wider and shaded by big trees and five-foot ways	More or less similar condition to the pedestrian environment today	Not friendly pedestrian environment—lack of wide sidewalks and shade
9 How safe was Kuala Lumpur 40 years ago	The place felt safer than the city today—much less crime	More or less similar to the condition today	It was less safer than the city today
10 What were the traffic jams like 40 years ago	Much less traffic jams than today	More or less similar to the current situation	There were worse traffic jams than today
11 What was the access to basic goods and services (shops, medical facilities, commercial and government institutions) like 40 years ago	Better than today	More or less similar	Worse than today
12 How was Kuala Lumpur managed in terms of waste collection and air quality 40 years ago	It was cleaner than the city today and the air quality was better	More or less similar condition to the one today	The city was more dirty than today and the air quality was worse

5   Urban and social infrastructure

Introduction

Kuala Lumpur's primary goal is to achieve a World Class City status by 2025. One of the major challenges ahead for the local authority and the federal government is to upgrade the city's urban and social infrastructure, which in some instances still resembles a 'third world environment'.

Lehman (2010) identifies 15 principles of an ideal sustainable and green urban environment. Four of these principles directly refer to urban infrastructure. They include zero-waste city, energy efficiency, sustainable water management and quality public transport. Three of the principles of affordable housing, public health and education address the social infrastructure issues.

This chapter focuses on the urban infrastructure, including water supply and wastewater distribution, waste management, energy supply, public transport and road network. It also discusses major social infrastructure, including hospitals and medical clinics, schools and tertiary education, cultural hubs and affordable housing. It traces the infrastructure of Kuala Lumpur developed from its beginning until the present. The political and social intentions that underpin the urban and social infrastructure and how these infrastructures are used are examined. There is also a critical analysis of the infrastructure using guidelines for inclusive urban infrastructure investments and criteria for social infrastructure in sustainable communities. Recreational and sports facilities, including local parks, stadiums and sports complexes, have been covered in Chapter 4; therefore, they are not discussed in this chapter.

This chapter also discusses the privatisation of urban infrastructure services in the Kuala Lumpur Metropolitan Region. The region has witnessed a gradual take-over of the essential municipal services by semi-private agencies. In addition, the chapter focuses on the rise of private medical establishments. The study explains the reasons for developing a sophisticated road network at the expense of a cutting-edge public transit system or innovative and efficient waste disposal.

Background: the definition and basic characteristics of urban and social infrastructures

Social and urban infrastructure includes the basic facilities, services and installations needed for the functioning of a community or society, such as transportation and communications systems, water and power lines, and public institutions, including schools, post offices and community centres (Free Dictionary, 2018).

The critical elements of the urban infrastructure include water supply, sewerage, waste collections, electricity and gas supply, the road network system, the public transport system and telecommunications, including the internet. Carmona et al. (2010) define the term capital web and argue that it is made of the above and below ground elements of the city's infrastructure. The above-ground level infrastructures include the road and the footpath network, and the public transport network, although part of it can be underground. Below ground infrastructure incorporates water supply network, the sewerage disposal system, electric grids, gas supply networks, telephone and internet cable networks. The car parking and loading service areas can be located underground or above ground.

Social Infrastructure is a subset of the infrastructure sector and typically includes assets that accommodate social services. Examples of social infrastructure include primary and secondary schools, universities, childcare centres, hospitals, medical centres, tertiary institutions, community centres. Social Infrastructure does not typically extend to the provision of social services, such as the provision of teachers at a school (NZSIF, 2018).

The development of urban infrastructure in Kuala Lumpur

This section discusses the essential urban infrastructure services in Kuala Lumpur, namely water supply, wastewater management, waste management, public transport, the road network, energy supply and telecommunications.

Water supply and waste water management

The piped water system was introduced in Kuala Lumpur by the British in the 19th century, and at the beginning of the 20th century, majority of households in Kuala Lumpur had piped water connection. However, it was not treated until 1906 when the first sand filter plant was built at the Ampang intake. Until the early 1990s, distribution and supply of water in Kuala Lumpur and Selangor, as well as the rest of Malaysia, was in the hands of the respective state governments. The gradual change took place in the 1990s when Malaysia embarked on the privatisation of water supply services and wastewater management. In 1996, Syarikat Bekalan Air Selangor Sdn. Bhd (SYABAS) was formed. The role of SYABAS is to supply water in Selangor, and the Federal Territories of Kuala Lumpur and Putrajaya, which covers a majority of the Kuala Lumpur Metropolitan Region. The company offers water for domestic, commercial and industrial customers (Pigeon, 2012; Bloomberg, 2018).

Investments in wastewater management experienced a slow pace after independence. Therefore, the responsibility for sewerage in much of Peninsular Malaysia was transferred from local governments to Indah Water Konsortium (IWK) in 1994. Current IWK is totally owned by the federal government. The main objective of IKW is to deliver a proper and efficient sewerage system and ensure that wastewater is sufficiently treated before it is discharged to the rivers (Indah Water Konsortium, 2018).

Kuala Lumpur has been successful in flood alleviation schemes. A master plan for flood mitigation in the entire Klang Valley was prepared by the Federal Department of Irrigation and Drainage. In conjunction with the Federal Government, the local authority developed a Kuala Lumpur Drainage Master Plan, and as a result, several flood mitigation schemes have been implemented. The most innovative flood mitigation project was the Storm-water Management and Road SMART Tunnel along the Klang River. The 3-km long road SMART tunnel opened in 2007. It is situated on top of a 9.7-km storm-water diversion tunnel (Morshidi and Abdul Rahim, 2010). Despite the success in the field of flood mitigation, flash flooding is still frequent in the Kuala Lumpur agglomeration. This is a result of the open drain system, which is vulnerable to any intense rainfalls.

Waste management

In 2008, a new government agency Solid Waste and Public Cleansing Management Corporation (PPSPPA) dealing in the solid waste management was formed. As a result, the responsibilities of solid waste and public cleansing management along with other related matters has been transferred from all the local authorities to PPSPPA now known as SWCorp (The Solid Waste Management and Public Cleansing Corporation). The roles of SWCorp are to ensure that the management of solid waste and public cleansing become more efficiently integrated and also in providing more satisfaction to consumers in delivering the service of solid waste and public cleansing management. Recently SWCorp has been active in imposing on residents in the Kuala Lumpur Metropolitan Region to separate their waste. Currently, Kuala Lumpur generates 3,000 tons of waste per day and is dependent on landfill sites outside its boundary. Today all the non–recyclable waste is sent to the transfer station at Taman Beringin and subsequently sent to Bukit Tagar sanitary landfill site. The goal of the KL City Plan is to achieve a recycling rate of 40% by 2020. Mandatory separation of recycled and non-recycled waste is also to be achieved by 2020 (DBKL, 2016).

Public transport

Car ownership in KL is the highest in Malaysia with over 90% household owning a car. Motor vehicle emissions are the leading cause of pollution in KL. While road transportation continues to be the dominant mode of transport, public transport is gradually becoming more popular and will be an essential feature in KL growth (SPAD, 2018b).

Historically, the public transport system in Kuala Lumpur started as a private sector initiative using buses. Introduced in 1995, the KTM Komuter was the first public transport mode operating in the already developing metropolitan region. The service works with two lines, namely the Seremban – Batu Caves Line and the Tanjung Malim – Pelabuhan Klang Line (SPAD, 2018c).

Light Rail was introduced to Kuala Lumpur in 1998 creating the first section of an automatic mass transit system in the city, running from east to west across the central parts of the city. The KL LRT was built to cater for the 1998 Commonwealth Games held in Kuala Lumpur. The LRT operates in Kuala Lumpur and also parts of Petaling Jaya (Transcore, 2017).

In 2002, Express Rail Link SdnBhd (ERL) launched its two flagship services, the KLIA Express and KLIA Transit which are high-speed rail services linking within the Multi-media Super Corridor linking

Kuala Lumpur with Putrajaya/Cyberjaya and the new Kuala Lumpur International Airport in Sepang. By its 10th year of operations in 2012, ERL had transported over 40 million passengers and today, continue to provide convenient, accessible and speedy travel options to its passengers (SPAD, 2018d).

An elevated monorail system connecting the major nodes of central Kuala Lumpur was opened in 2004. The 8.5-km long KL Monorail is an intercity public transit system that links many key destinations within Kuala Lumpur's busiest central commercial, employment and shopping districts (SPAD, 2018a).

The Land Public Transport Commission (SPAD) was established on 3rd June 2010, following the passing of the Suruhanjaya Pengangkutan Awam Darat Act 2010 by the Parliament on May 2010. The Commission gained its full authority on 31st January 2011 with the gazetting of the Land Public Transport Act 2010 (SPAD, 2018a).

In 2017, the Kuala Lumpur MRT Sungai Buloh-Kajang Line was opened. It is a fully automatic public transit rail service that connects the city centre to various neighbourhoods in Kuala Lumpur and edge cities within the KLMR including Sungai Buloh, Kajang. The MRT line features 31 stations along its 51-km long route, each of which are fitted with convenient facilities such as lifts and ramps for the disabled, escalators, customer service centres, ticket vending machines, prayer rooms, and toilets (Kuala Lumpur MRT SBK Line). The construction of the MRT Line 2 for the Sungai Buloh-Serdang-Putrajaya is currently underway. The MRT Line 2 will serve a corridor with a population of around 2 million stretching from Sungai Buloh via Central Business District of Kuala Lumpur to Bandar Malaysia, Kuchai Lama and Serdang before ending at Cyberjaya and Putrajaya. The 52.2-km line will include a 13.5-km underground section in the central parts of Kuala Lumpur and 38.7 km of the viaduct. There will be 37 stations, 26 of which will be elevated with 11 underground stations (SPAD, 2018b).

In recent years, Malaysia government has placed a higher priority in resource allocation to public transport to improve mobility in KL. Based on the government's approved public transport infrastructure, it has envisaged that public transport will have a modal share of 40% by 2030. It seeks to persuade riders of the public to switch from private vehicles to public transportation. It is now the asset owner and operator of the stage bus and light metro services in KL.

The new MRT line is shown in Figure 5.1a and b.

(a) (b)

Figure 5.1 The new MRT line Sungai Buloh-Kajang- the car (a, left) and the one of the new MRT stations (b, right).
Source: M. Kozlowski.

The road network

In Malaysia, road constructions had begun since before independence. However, after the country gained independence in 1957, efforts to improve the road system had always been placed high on the political agenda. Every 5 years, the Malaysia Plan launched by the Federal Government emphasises on the importance of road construction (Malaysian Roads, 2018). Construction of roads in Malaysia was implemented mainly by the Federal Government and State Governments. However, since the mid-1980s, development of toll highways has been introduced by private companies. These private companies are authorized by the government to charge tolls to road users (Malaysian Roads, 2018).

Road construction in the Kuala Lumpur-Klang Region also has undergone through a privatisation process. Under the privatization policy, the road building program for the Klang Valley set out in the KLSP 1984, which comprised 23 new roads and 21 major road improvement projects, together with some additional toll highways has mostly been completed by 2010. The road network now in place has succeeded in its primary purposes of eliminating through traffic from the City Centre, reducing congestion on minor roads and efficiently dispersing traffic from the City Centre (DBKL, 2012).

Between 1985 and 1997, the modal share of public transport in the KL-Klang Region has decreased from 34.3% to 19.7%. This represents a significant shift away from public transport and in particular bus transport, which is partly attributable to higher personal affluence leading to an increase in car ownership and also to deficiencies in the bus services. The increasing reliance on private transportation, in particular, private cars, has created considerable pressure on the road network, which has contributed to the problems of traffic congestion (DBKL, 2012).

The current road network, including the major highways', criss-crosses the metropolitan region making the car the most convenient way of getting around. Besides, subsidised petrol prices and cheap or even free parking encourage people to choose cars as a preferred transport mode. According to Mahirah et al. (2015) the rapid surge of car ownership contributed to the enormous traffic congestion in the Kuala Lumpur conurbation. Many parts of KLMR still do not have proper access to public transport modes. As a result, the traffic congestion is worsening every year, and the opening of the new MRT line in 2017 only in a small fraction reduced the problem.

In Kuala Lumpur various traffic control and monitoring measures have been successfully implemented The principal means of traffic control in the City presently comprises a computer-based area traffic signal coordination system that operates 130 intersections, supplemented by the traffic police during peak hours. Extension of the existing traffic control system, together with an upgrading of the system's capability, is currently being implemented in phases (DBKL, 2012).

Pedestrian and cycling network

The Urban Guidelines for Kuala Lumpur City Centre (DBKL, 2014) identified poor pedestrian connectivity between major activity nodes of the central city. Majority of the streetscapes in the central city are dominated by car parking, poor quality architecture, extensive carriageways, lack of tree planting and in many instances the dominance of above-ground public utility installations. The area can be described as an unwelcoming sea of car parking spaces and traffic congestion, which has a detrimental impact on the street quality environment. The existing footpaths are not pedestrian-friendly as most of them are either too narrow and lack any shading devices in the form of awnings or canopy tree planting. Jalan Ampang and Jalan P. Ramlee, the Bintang Walk along Jalan Sultan Ismail are the few pedestrian-friendly street environments in central Kuala Lumpur.

Air transport

The first airport introducing air travel to Kuala Lumpur was opened in Sungai Besi in 1952. In 1965 the airport was moved to Subang which became the Kuala Lumpur International Airport until 1998. In 1998 majority of the international services were transferred from Subang to the new Kuala Lumpur International Airport in Sepang built as part of the 1998 Commonwealth Games infrastructure. Subang still services like an airport until today catering for budget airlines and mainly domestic services (Subang International Airport, 2018).

The Kuala Lumpur International Airport (KLIA) is situated in Sepang, about 50 km away from Kuala Lumpur City Centre. The airport serves international and domestic flights via its three terminals, KLIA Main Terminal Building (MTB), Satellite Terminal A and KLIA2. The latter terminal services mainly low budget airlines such as Air Asia. Travellers may move back and forth between MTB and KLIA 2 via a high-speed train known as the Express Rail Link (ERL) or the KLIA Express, and the journey takes about three minutes. MTB and Satellite Terminal A are connected by a sky bridge and an Aerotrain, which travels back and forth in about five minutes. KLIA is connected to Putrajaya/Cyberjaya and Sentral KL by the Express Rail Link (ERL). The journey to central Kuala Lumpur takes around 30 minutes. Both KLIA terminals catered for 59 million passengers in 2018 (Skyscanner, 2019).

The airport's design focuses on the environment, with a spotlight on greenery. The Satellite Building features an entire area of natural rainforest and KLIA is the first airport in the world to be awarded the Green Globe 21 certificate for pledging to champion environmental answerability.

KLIA for the past two decades serves as the primary international gateway to Kuala Lumpur and Malaysia.

Energy supply

Electricity supply in the Kuala Lumpur regional is provided through a national grid which covers all of Peninsular Malaysia. It is operated and owned by Tenaga Nasional Berhad (TNB).

The history of electricity in Kuala Lumpur goes back to 1895 when the railway stations in the city received their electricity supply. The first electricity board was established in 1949. After gaining independence in 1957, the new government placed a strong emphasis on developing electricity in Selangor.

In 1965, the Central Electricity Board was replaced with the National Electricity Board and the plans to develop a national electricity grid in Peninsular Malaysia were set into motion. The National Grid is the primary electricity transmission network linking the electricity generation, transmission, distribution and consumption in Peninsular Malaysia. The power generating plants were strategically located in each state. The National Grid was finally completed in the early 1980s.

In 1984, Prime Minister Dato Seri Dr Mahathir Mohamad announced the government's decision to privatise the National Grid, which was completed in 1990 with the establishment of a new private corporation called Tenaga National Berhad (Tenaga National Berhad, 2018).

Another significant body in coordinating the management of energy supply in Malaysia, including Kuala Lumpur is the Energy Commission. It is responsible for regulating the energy sector, specifically the electricity and piped gas supply industries, in Peninsular Malaysia and Sabah (Energy Commission Malaysia, 2018).

The goal of the local authority and Federal Government is to achieve better energy efficiency. Attaining energy efficiency through planning and design measures is elaborated in the 'A Greener Better Kuala Lumpur Report'. The planning measures included a more compact urban form and provision of walkable and cycling-friendly urban districts. The Report also focuses on energy efficiency, examining measures that should be undertaken in the foreseeable future. The measures include implementing a new sustainable energy management system supported by a net metering system, development of a 'smart grid', implementing an online energy monitoring system, and optimising the use for renewable and more alternative energy including solar energy, waste to energy and developing more advanced energy systems (DBKL, 2016).

At present, renewable sources used to generate electricity include hydro, biomass, biogas, wind energy and solar energy. Wind energy has grown strongly over recent years, especially in Scandinavian countries. However, because of the lack of permanent wind gusts in the Greater Kuala Lumpur area, wind energy is not a recommended solution. Emerging renewable energy technologies that are yet to be commercially deployed include large-scale solar energy plants and geothermal generation technologies.

Cities around the world are switching to LED lights as a way to save both money and energy while simultaneously increasing safety and visibility. Replacing traditional mercury street lights with LED lighting is the most feasible solution to achieve energy savings. Similar to the trends in other global cities the immediate action that can take place in urban districts and public spaces of Kuala Lumpur is the replacement of the traditional lighting system with a more long term and efficient LED lighting.

Telecommunications

There are no specific statistics regarding telecommunications in the KL-Klang region as the broadband, and mobile networks are offered by private national providers. The three leading mobile private providers include Celcom, Maxis and Digi, while the national broadband is provided by Telekom Malaysia. According to independent research University, Malaya (2012) telecommunications has evolved rapidly in the past 20 years with the number of mobile phone subscribers reached 33 million in 2010, which surpassed the national population number. Growth in the telecom industry was triggered by liberalization, the introduction of competition, the advancement of technology, and the facilitative policy and regulatory efforts of the government to promote and initiate telecommunications investments (University of Malaya, 2018).

National broadband in Malaysia is provided by Telekom Malaysia Berhad (TM) with a history dating back to 1946. TM is Malaysia's converged communications services provider offering a comprehensive range of communication services and solutions in broadband, mobility, wifi and smart services. Following the neoliberal trends and privatisation of infrastructure, TM was privatised in the late 1980s (Telekom Malaysia, 2018).

Being the major urban conurbation of Malaysia, the KLMR is one of the leading digital urban centres of Southeast Asia.

The development of social infrastructure in Kuala Lumpur

Hospital and medical clinics

Similar to the rest of Malaysia, Kuala Lumpur and its urban conurbation have a dual-tiered system of healthcare services: a government-led and public-funded sector and a thriving private sector. According to Qeuk (2014), during the Mahathir period from 1981 to 2003, the number of beds in private hospitals increased by tenfold. A review of ten best hospitals in the city of Kuala Lumpur revealed that six of them are private hospitals with lucrative private medical centres, such as Prince Court Medical Centre, Pantai Medical Centre and Gleneagles Hospital, topping the list (Kuala Lumpur Health and Medical Hospitals, 2018).

As a result of the rapid rise of the private health sector industry, Malaysia is making a mark in the health tourism industry and becoming one of the leading health tourism destinations of the ASEAN region (The Star Online, 2019).

As a result of the rapid rise of private health care, Malaysia is ranked high in terms of the quality of the health industry and services.

Figure 5.2 Prince Court Medical Centre a private upmarket hospital.
Source: M. Kozlowski.

According to the International Living website among top six countries that obtained the best ratings in the category of Best Healthcare in the World for this year, Malaysia ranked first with its world-class healthcare services and sophisticated infrastructure (The Star Online, 2019).

The luxurious private hospital -Prince Court Medical Centre is shown in Figure 5.2.

Primary and secondary schools

Education in Malaysia may be obtained from the public school system, which provides free education for all Malaysians regardless of ethnic background. There are private and international schools that require fees. By law, primary education in Malaysia is compulsory. The Ministry of Education oversees the primary and secondary education system in Kuala Lumpur. Each state and territory in Malaysia has its education department to monitor and coordinate educational matters. A majority of the schools in Kuala Lumpur Metropolitan Region are monitored by the Selangor Educational Department. The major

school types in the KLMR include government primary and secondary schools, Chinese primary and secondary public schools and
Chinese private independent schools (Edarabia, 2018).

According to Emerging Strategy (2016), Malaysia's growth of private
school enrolment in the past decade is enormous. It grew from less than
1% in 2002 to 15% in 2013 and 17% in 2016 and is expected to continue
rising. This rapid growth is driven by the soaring demand for private
and international schools catering to the needs of urban middle classes.

There are as much as 76 private international schools in Kuala
Lumpur. These schools cater to various nationalities and offer a range of
international curricula (Expat Arrivals, 2018). The rise of international
schools in Malaysia is being driven by government efforts to reform education. Since the government considers international schools an engine
of economic transformation, it removed the limits on foreign ownership of international schools, introduced tax incentives, and removed
the 40% enrolment cap for Malaysian students. Furthermore, to transform Malaysia into an educational hub, the government has invested in
large-scale projects such as The New Kuala Lumpur Education City.
Prestigious international schools have been invited to open locations,
which will likely raise the number of Malaysian students enrolling in
international schools in the next few years (Emerging Strategy, 2016).

There is strong traction that private religious schools have achieved
in recent years. In 2005 there were 20 private religious primary schools
and 15 such secondary schools. Within a decade the numbers grew to
43 primary schools and 74 secondary schools. The growth of private
schooling in emerging markets is a direct response from rising middle
classes to their governments' failure to provide quality education for the
21st-century economy, and this trend is likely to continue. Malaysia has
supported international schools to propel economic growth (Emerging
Strategy, 2016; Afterschool High Education Advisor, 2018b).

Tertiary education

Traditionally, tertiary education in Malaysia was under the patronage
and responsibility of the federal and state governments. However, in
the last two decades, there is an explosion of private universities. Based
on a cursory review of the list of universities in Malaysia, there are currently six major public universities operating in KLMR. These universities include, University Malaya, University Putra Malaysia, University
Technology Mara (UiTM). University Technology Malaysia, University Kebangsaan Malaysia (UKM), University Islam Antrabangsa
Malaysia (UIAM) and University Pertahanan National Malaysia.

However, in comparison, there are 52 private universities and private university colleges and also, seven foreign universities which total to 59 private tertiary educational establishments operating in the entire KL metropolitan region (Afterschool High Education Advisor, 2018a; Study Malaysia, 2018). The figures above reveal that there an absolute over-dominance of private educational institutions in Kuala Lumpur and the surrounding urban conurbation. Some universities are mainly aimed at targeting foreign students. For example, Limkokwing University campus in Cyberjaya caters for 30,000 students from 165 countries (Limkokwing University, 2018). Xiamen University in Sepang is the first Chinese university in Malaysia, targeting students from mainland China and Taiwan (Xiamen University, 2019). Private universities and colleges have an open policy regarding recruitment of academic staff. The public universities have always had a policy of strongly favouring Malay/Bumiputra academics (Hunter, 2019). It should be noted that one of the major public universities University Technology Mara (UiTM) is open exclusively to Bumiputra students only.

View of newly built private Herriot Watt University building is shown in Figure 5.3.

Figure 5.3 Private Herriot Watt University Complex in Putrajaya.
Source: M. Kozlowski.

Cultural hubs

There are 15 museums in the city of Kuala Lumpur with the National Museum (Museum Negara) and the Islamic Arts Museum topping the list. Each of the major satellite cities within the urban conurbation such as Petaling Jaya or Shah Alam has its own local museum (Inspirok, 2018).

According to Trip Advisor (2018), there are 17 arts performing complexes and live theatres in Kuala Lumpur. The major ones include the Performing Arts Complex in Sentul, The Concert Hall in the Convention Centre and the Istana Budaya Theatre. The Istana Budaya is also known as the Palace of Culture, is Malaysia's leading venue for all types of theatre including musical theatre, operetta, classical concerts and opera from local and international performances. It is located in the heart of Kuala Lumpur city, next to the Taman Titiwangsa (Titiwangsa Park).

There are five major public libraries in Kuala Lumpur and Selangor, including the Kuala Lumpur Library and the National Library of Malaysia (ExpatGo, 2018). According to The Adult and Youth Literacy: National Regional and Global Trends report published in 2016, 85% of Malaysians who read regularly, however, 77% prefer newspapers, and only three per read printed books. This low reading habit is attributed mainly to the rise of technology and changing trends with people and students, moving away from printed books to electronic, digital, web and social media platforms (New Straight Times, 2018). However, reading habit among Malaysians are substantially lower than western countries (39% of Americans and 67% of Germans read printed books on regular basis). This is the main reason why there is not an established network of local public libraries in urban localities throughout Malaysia (Publishing Perspectives, 2018).

The thousands of Mosques and Surau's located in the Kuala Lumpur Metropolitan Region, not only function as a place to perform prayers but also serve as multifunctional space to conduct various activities involving individual and communal needs. Mosques are often regarded as main community centres of diverse residential neighbourhoods. Mosques in urban Malaysia always serve to address the needs of the Muslim community (Baharudin and Ismail, 2015).

There are also 82 Christian churches located in KLMR that cater to the local Christian communities and also act as places of social interaction (Archdiocese of Kuala Lumpur, 2019).

Affordable housing

The last two decades have witnessed a massive surge of property prices in Malaysia, especially in the Kuala Lumpur – Klang Region. According to Zainon et al. (2017), the majority of medium income earners in Kuala Lumpur and Selangor do not qualify for social housing and are not able to afford private sector housing.

To address housing for the growing middle-income groups, the Federal Government and private developers came with a response by establishing several housing programs. The programs include 1Peoples's Malaysia Housing Program (PR1MA), 1 Malaysia Civil Servant Housing Program (PPA1M), Rumah Mesra Rakyat 1 Malaysia (RMR1M), People's Housing Project (PPR), My Home Federal Territory Affordable Housing Policy (RUMAWIP) and Rumah Selangorku (Zainon et al., 2017).

Perbadanan PR1MA Malaysia was established under the PR1MA Act 2012 to plan, develop, construct and maintain high-quality housing with lifestyle concepts for middle-income households in key urban centres.

Homes developed by PR1MA are priced between RM100,000 to RM400,000, giving opportunities to average income workers to own their own home. Earmarked for development in key strategic urban areas nationwide, PR1MA is open to all Malaysians with a monthly household income between RM2, 500 to RM15,000. PR1MA has developed a few major residential projects in the Kuala Lumpur Metropolitan Area (PR1MA, 2018).

In terms of social housing for the low-income groups, the National Housing Department (Jabatan Perumahan Negara or JPN) has launched the Peoples Housing Project Program (Perumahan Rakyat or PPR). This housing program for the poor is well established in Kuala Lumpur and the surrounding metropolitan region (Tee et al., 2011) Under the Peoples Housing Program people of low income can rent or buy houses built by the federal or state governments at a low rate (Borneo Post, 2018).

As a result of state and federal government initiatives and housing programs, squatter housing has been almost totally eradicated from Kuala Lumpur and the surrounding metropolitan region (DBKL, 2012).

Security, emergency and social welfare facilities

The security and emergency services in KLMR include national police headquarters, police posts, district police headquarters, neighbourhood watch centres and fire stations. The Police Department is under the jurisdiction of the Ministry of Home Affairs, while the Fire Brigade is the responsibility of the Ministry of Housing and Local Government.

Kuala Lumpur and the entire region is gradually becoming an age-` ing urban conurbation. In 2000, 6% of the population were 60 and above. No official statistics have been produced since then; however, following the national trends that figure could have almost doubled by today. There were over 10,000 disabled persons register in Kuala Lumpur in 2000; today the percentage of disabled in Kuala Lumpur is nearly double the national average (Malaysia Department of Statistics, 2018). To combat these growing trends the Federal Territory's Department of Social Welfare and Islamic Council for the Federal Territory manages welfare centres and coordinates social welfare programs (DBKL, 2012).

Critical analysis

Urban infrastructure

This section will analyse the performance of existing urban and social infrastructures against a set of recognised principles and best practices for sustainable and inclusive infrastructure.

Cities Development Initiatives for Asia (CDIA) (2017) indicate that clean cities with quality urban infrastructure are an essential ingredient of business-friendly urban environments. The provision of quality urban infrastructure stimulates economic growth and development of cities. For an inclusive city, the link between residential population and urban infrastructure is critical for wellbeing and proper functioning of the city (CDIA, 2017).

Water supply, sewerage and drainage are inclusive when they are safe, and services are available to all members of the community. Lehman (2010) argues that one of the main principles of a sustainable green city is closed urban water management and high water quality. The author further asserts that the city can be used as a water catchment area with full stormwater and rainwater collection. Wastewater recycling and storm-water harvesting have to be introduced. On a household level, it is imperative to have a dual water reticulation system where rainwater and greywater can be fully utilised and recycled. Kuala Lumpur and its metropolitan region have an abundance of rainfall and semi-privatisation of water supply, and wastewater management has improved the overall system. However, the existing open drain system struggles with frequent downpours and flash-flooding is common. Although 70% of residents in Kuala Lumpur are connected to a reticulated sewerage system, a significant proportion of the urban area remain still unconnected. Majority of the wastewater is cleaned and discharged back to the environment and not being utilised for any other purpose (DBKL, 2016). Kuala Lumpur and other major cities in Malaysia lose millions of gallons of water annually as a result of leakages in the distribution pipes (DBKL, 2016). In terms of achieving sustainable water and water-waste management system, Kuala Lumpur has a long way to go. Although there has been an on-going discourse on the notion of smart water management, including recycling of storm-water and wastewater and the introduction of information and communication technologies (ICT), no action has yet been undertaken.

Inclusive energy must provide services and accessibility for all residents in the urban areas (CDIA, 2017). A fully sustainable city should be a self-sufficient on-site energy producer using decentralised district energy systems (Lehman, 2010).

According to the Suruhanjaya Tenaga (Energy Commission Malaysia) (2017), over 87% of energy in Malaysia is still produced from non-recyclable sources, including gas and coal. This figure is significantly higher than leading Western European countries where currently almost 50% of energy derives from renewable sources. Kuala Lumpur has always aspired to transform into a low carbon city, including the promotion of renewable energy sources. However, the reality is different, and the local authorities together with the federal government and relevant stakeholders have a long way ahead to harmonise the existing commercial and industrial sectors with the sustainable energy consumption practices (DBKL, 2016).

According to DBKL (2016), the current energy consumption of a postmodern urban environment like Kuala Lumpur is not sustainable with high carbon emissions from the centralised power generation mechanism. The development of a more sustainable energy system promoting more efficient energy consumption and renewable energy options for townships, urban districts and public spaces is necessary.

The Green Building Index (GBI) Township rating system addresses energy efficiency in urban townships and districts. It seeks to promote the development of townships that are well-planned and designed to enhance the surrounding environment, thus providing a high quality of life for the residents. Out of 18 total registered green township projects, 9 township developments have been granted certification as at March 2017. In particular, Tun Razak Exchange (township) was certified as under the platinum category, the highest classification under the GBI (Green Building Index Malaysia, 2019).

The inefficient waste collection could create a detrimental effect on the urban environment, resulting in health risks and increased pollution. Organic waste dominates the waste composition in Malaysian cities, including Kuala Lumpur (DBKL, 2016). All organic waste is currently dumped at landfill sites, which significantly contribute to greenhouse gas emissions (GHG). Recycled waste is only partially reused and utilised. Although recyclable and non-recyclable waste bins have been distributed in public areas within the Kuala Lumpur agglomeration, the domestic waste collection is still based on a traditional non-segregation system in the majority of the metropolitan region. Separation of recyclable and non recyclable domestic waste has only been achieved in the Federal Territory of Putrajaya. In Malaysia, including the Kuala Lumpur agglomeration, there are no specific policies for recycling of commercial waste generated from all premises used for business purposes. As a result, there are no guidelines on how to manage commercial organic waste such as wasted food, and recycled waste including paper, plastics and metals. Another critical element of waste management is an electronic waste collection generated from electrical or electronic equipment. There are no specific policies on e-waste management, although several pilot projects have been conducted in central parts of Kuala Lumpur (DBKL, 2016). One of the principle guidelines for sustainable waste management is the development of a circular closed-loop management system where all organic and non-organic waste is reused and recycled (Lehman, 2010). Waste management in Kuala Lumpur and its metropolitan region operate still on a traditional linear system with waste being collected and the majority of it discharged at selected landfill sites. Morshidi and Abdul Rahman indicated in 2010 that the waste management system in Kuala Lumpur is not sufficient. Recent observations carried out in selected areas of the metropolitan region revealed that only semi-privatised precincts such as KLCC and the administrative capital of Putrajaya are relatively clean, however, in other urban areas litter is distributed at random. There is an urgent need to educate the inhabitants of the KLMR and even, following the example of Singapore, consider introducing penalties for littering in the public areas. Currently, waste management in the KLMR and elsewhere in Malaysia is coordinated by several different entities. Domestic waste management falls under the jurisdiction of the Ministry of Housing, industrial waste is monitored by the Ministry of Energy, Science, Technology, Environment and

Climate Change and commercial waste are controlled by respective local authorities.

For cities with world-class ambitions, it is imperative to have a green well-functioning public transit system accessible and available to all citizens. The 2016 Greener Better Report Kuala Lumpur Report promotes green mobility as integration of light rail, monorail, rapid mass transit, bus service and bicycle network (DBKL, 2016). Lehman (2010) discusses the concept of eco-mobility emphasising strongly on integrated transport systems and the provision of supporting bicycle and pedestrian-friendly environments. The public transport system has is being developed in the KLMR since 1998. Currently, the public transport system in KLMR is regarded as one of the most advanced in the ASEAN region, falling only behind the one in Singapore. However, public transport is still not available in many urban areas, and a lot of residential neighbourhoods and commercial centres are located at a significant distance away from the transport hubs. Besides, there is a lack of a feeder bus network supporting the light rail and mass rapid transit. The bike network and pedestrian network linking to the primary transport also have not been developed. Even the planned administrative capital Putrajaya, although very well connected to central Kuala Lumpur and the Kuala Lumpur International Airport by a fast train, has no efficient public transport system linking the 20 precincts of the city. This situation makes Putrajaya an almost totally car-dependent environment. There is an existing bus network system operated by Nadi Putra Bus Service; however, the system has limited connections between various precincts and also a low trip frequency.

In the last 30 years, the KLMR has developed an adequate road network system with multiple lane highways linking all the major centres of the urban conurbation. The road network was developed in parallel with a rapid rise of private car ownership strongly supported by the Federal Government. Lehman (2010) argues that more and broader roads result in an increased car and truck traffic and CO_2 emissions, which triggers further urban sprawl. This phenomenon is taking place in the KLMR region with increased traffic congestion even though the public transport system has also been expanded. Besides, the local authorities in the metropolitan region have not been discouraging the use of cars. Low parking fees are an additional stimulus for people to use their vehicles. Recently DBKL has abolished the clamping of illegally parked cars which immediately triggered at- random parking on the streets of Kuala Lumpur including the major heavily trafficked roads.

The Urban Design Guidelines for Kuala Lumpur Central City identified seven street typologies for the city centre. The Guidelines include detailed design solutions for each street typology aimed at improving the street ambience and creating a pedestrian-friendly environment. The design solutions include extending the footpaths and providing canopy trees to create thermal comfort. The additional design criteria for streets are the inclusion of shading devices such as collonades and awnings that should be incorporated to offer solar protection during the days (DBKL, 2014). Four years after the endorsement of the Urban Design Guidelines improvement works have commenced in Masjid India along Jalan Tuanku Abdul Rahman and around Masjid Jamek and Pasar Seni (the Central Market) in the catchment area of the River of Life project.

Social infrastructure

Brown and Barber (2017) identified social equity (access to key services, facilities and opportunities including employment, transportation and affordable housing), social cohesion/inclusion and social capital (measured by such indicators as happiness, wellbeing and quality of life) as the key determinants of good social infrastructure.

Lehman (2010) indicates that the provision of affordable housing should be a priority for all municipal authorities. He suggests that a cap should be imposed requesting all private residential developments to provide at least 40% of affordable housing, which will be integrated with the private accommodation. He further indicates that mixed-use development delivers more social inclusion and helps to repopulate the city centre. Brown and Barber (2017) argue that promoting planning that addresses scale, local context, diversified building types and long term stable urban governance are the key elements in achieving a well-functioning and sustainable social infrastructure. It is imperative that the majority of social services, including schools, community centres, medical centres and hospitals, are accessible to all members of the community and located within the residential areas. Llewelyn Davies (2000) quotes that

> A successful and sustainable local neighbourhood is a product of the distances people have to walk to access daily facilities, the presence of a sufficient range of such facilities to support their needs, and places and spaces where a variety of activities can take place.
>
> (Llewelyn-Davies, 2000, p. 39)

Cultural hubs are also an essential part of the urban landscape, which gives the city its specific cultural identity. According to the UNESCO global report on culture and the future of urban areas, culture lies at the heart of sustainable policies and has a significant influence on urban development. The report promotes strongly cultural regeneration as an adequate tool for cities that have gone through big economic changes and as a result need to promote local culture and activity to regain its lost sense of identity (UNESCO, 2016).

The social infrastructure is only marginally addressed in the newly gazetted 2020 Local KL City Plan with a small section dedicated to public facilities. The Plan has earmarked all existing and planned public facilities sites in the city of Kuala Lumpur based on a targeted population of 2.2 million by 2030. The Plan envisages that additional community facilities will be secured through new developments or redevelopment projects (DBKL, 2018).

However, it has been substantially addressed in KL 2020 Structure Plan with an entire section focusing on educational facilities, health facilities, welfare facilities and cultural hubs. The distribution of public educational facilities in Kuala Lumpur and the surrounding region is undertaken by the Ministry of Education in collaboration with local councils including DBKL. According to DBKL in 2012 childcare centres, primary and secondary schools are not evenly distributed according to the population distribution in the city of Kuala Lumpur (DBKL, 2012).

Public health facilities in KLMR are provided by the Ministry of Health. Although the city of Kuala Lumpur has a wide range of health facilities from the general to the very specialised, in the last years' private clinic and hospitals, have taken over with more and more Malaysian subscribing to private medical health insurance. According to Querk (2014), the public health service caters for a bulk of the population (65%) but is served by 45% of registered doctors and only 25% of the specialists. The Malaysia private health care system is growing is now ranked as one of the best in the World (The Star Online, 2019). The existing trends in health care move Malaysia away from the traditional welfare health care systems of countries such as the United Kingdom where almost everybody benefits from the National Health Service, and the role of the private health sector is only marginal (Chang, 2019).

In modern intelligent and sustainable cities, it is essential that cultural facilities are accessible to all and located in central areas within the proximity of public transport modes. In Kuala Lumpur, the National Theatre (Istana Budaya), National Art Gallery, and the

National Library are located outside the city centre without proper public transport access. The new Kuala Lumpur Arts Performing Complex is located in Sentul, which is a few kilometers away from the heart of the city. Although the KLPAC is located within walking distance of the LRT and KTM stations, Sentul has never been recognized as a cultural precinct of the city. The distribution of cultural complexes within Kuala Lumpur is very fragmented and does not follow any logical pattern.

According to DBKL (2012), the police stations and police post are not evenly distributed according to population distribution. There are also an insufficient number of social welfare facilities.

Education experiencing rapid privatisation is gradually less accessible to the broader community. The bulk of universities and colleges in KLMR are privately owned with major groups such as the Sunway Group and Limkokwing having a major share in the higher education sector. In comparison, in the most prominent World City London out of 56 universities and higher education's institutions, only eight (8) are private (Study London, 2019; Study UK, 2019). The situation in KLMR is reverse with seven major public universities and 59 private universities and colleges. The public universities seem to be losing their prime position, although they still top the rankings because of their robust research component. However, there is no doubt that tertiary education in the KL region has been converted into a lucrative 'money-making' business. According to Hunter (2019), one year after the 2018 elections the situation in Malaysia public universities have not changed despite the pre-election promises of the current ruling Pakatan Harapan coalition to place education reform as one of their priorities. An attempt to develop an environment promoting strong international cooperation backed by critical and creative thinking has not occurred.

Major findings and conclusions

Neoliberalism emerged strongly in the late 1970s era characterised by stagnation and economic recession. It has powerfully influenced urban policies, especially in large global cities. One of the main precepts of neoliberalism was to give the private sector a leading role in the physical development of the cities. Deregulation, privatisation and withdrawal of state intervention were the fundamental objectives of this new trend in politics. This included the provision and operation of municipal services, including urban and social infrastructures (Purcell, 2011).

Since the 1990s Malaysia has followed the main precepts of neoliberalism and gradually privatised the necessary urban services. Neoliberalism began to take root during the two decades of administration under Prime Minister Mahathir Mohamad and was continued under Prime Ministers Abdullah Badawi and Najib Razak (Lim, 2017).

Neoliberalism had a profound impact on the urban development of KLMR since the early 1990s. Semi-privatisation of primary municipal services including waste and water management's energy supply, and telecommunication services follows the trends and practices of other major cities around the World. Public transport including the LRT, Monorail and MRT are the still fully subsidised by the government. Neoliberalism constituted a key strategy ensuring a partial government involvement in the maintenance and operation of the urban infrastructure services. However, the privatisation of the urban infrastructure has not created a faultless well-functioning system as power and water outages occur almost every year. The current water and waste management systems are still far away from achieving an enclosed sustainable loop where the majority of waste is recycled, and the grey and storm-water are fully reused. Although DBKL, the Federal and State Governments are fully committed to the introduction of sustainable urban infrastructure; the existing deliverables are limited to pilot projects and lengthy planning reports.

The social infrastructure in Kuala Lumpur Metropolitan Region is not working as a mediator between communities, and as a result, the social facilities being currently built are less inclusive targeting a specific income bracket. The health and education sectors have witnessed a fierce privatisation process even surpassing the famous 'Thatcherism privatisation period' in the United Kingdom in the 1980s and 1990s. The contemporary KLMR has become a beacon of private schools and tertiary education institutions as well as lucrative private medical clinics and hospitals.

Bibliography

Afterschool Higher Education Advisor (2018a) Top 14 Private Universities in Kuala Lumpur. https://afterschool.my/private-universities-in-kuala-lumpur

Afterschool Higher Education Advisor (2018b) 21 Private Colleges in Kuala Lumpur. https://afterschool.my/private-colleges-in-kuala-lumpur

Archdiocese of Kuala Lumpur (2019) https://archkl.org/index.php/en/

Baharudin, N. A., and Ismail, S. A. (2015) Architectural Style of Da'wah Mosque in Malaysia: From Vernacular to Modern Structures. *International Journal of Built Environment and Sustainability*, 3(2), 70–78. https://core.ac.uk/download/pdf/129878314.pdf

Bloomberg (2018) Company Overview of Syarikat Bekalan Air Selangor Sdn. Bhd (SYABAS). www.bloomberg.com/research/stocks/private/snapshot. asp?privcapid=13757267

Borneo Post (May 7, 2018) Ensuring all Malaysians have Quality Housing. www.pressreader.com/

Brown, J., and Barber, A. (2017) Social Infrastructure and Sustainable Urban Communities. *Engineering Sustainability*, 165(ES1), 99–109.

Carmona, M., Heath, T., Taner, O. C., and Tiesdell, S. (2010) *Public Spaces-Urban Spaces: The Dimensions of Urban Design*. Oxford: Architectural Press.

Chang, J., Peysakhovich, F., Wang, W., and Zhu, J. (2019) The UK Health Care System. http://assets.ce.columbia.edu/pdf/actu/actu-uk.pdf

Cities Development Initiatives for Asia (2017) *Inclusive Urban Infrastructure Investments: Guidelines for Municipalities*. Asia Development Bank Publication.

Dewan Bandaraya Kuala Lumpur (DBKL) (2008) Kuala Lumpur Structure Plan 2020.

Dewan Bandaraya Kuala Lumpur (DBKL) (2012) City Plan 2020.

Dewan Bandaraya Kuala Lumpur (DBKL) (2014) Urban Design Guidelines for Kuala Lumpur City Centre.

Dewan Bandaraya Kuala Lumpur (DBKL) (2016) A Greener Better Kuala Lumpur.

Dewan Bandaraya Kuala Lumpur (DBKL) (2018) Master Plan for Kuala Lumpur City Competitiveness.

Edarabia (2018) A List of 25 Best School in Kuala Lumpur. https://www. edarabia.com/schools/kuala-lumpur/

Emerging Strategy (2016) Malaysia's Government Policy Driving Rapid Growth of Private and International School Enrolment. www.emerging-strategy.com/article/rapid-growth-of-private-and-international-schools-in-malaysia-driven-by-government-policy-is-an-attractive-short-term-growth-opportunity/

Expat Arrivals (2018) International Schools in Kuala Lumpur. www. expatarrivals.com/asia-pacific/malaysia/kuala-lumpur/international-schools-kuala-lumpur

ExpatGo (2018) Public Libraries in Kuala Lumpur and Selangor. www.expatgo.com/my/2018/09/03/public-libraries-in-kl-and-selangor/

Free Dictionary (2018) Definition of Social Infrastructure. www.thefreedictionary.com/infrastructure

Green Building Index Malaysia (2019) GBI Tools. https://new.greenbuildingindex.org/

Hunter, M. (2019) Asia Sentinel: Malaysian Universities Are Still Going Backwards. https://www.asiasentinel.com/society/malaysia-public-universities-going-backwards/?fbclid=IwAR3jB7sLNSm4eAdwtyCrk-FZFJdSBLiT7X7auj7g59PJ5ZloNtYrIBj83wzg

Indah Water Konsortium (IKW) (2018) Company Profile. www.tnb.com.my/about-tnb/history/

Inspirok (2018) Museums in Kuala Lumpur. www.inspirock.com/malaysia/
museums-in-kuala-lumpur?ad_acc=iphk&gclid=Cj0KCQiAnNXiBRCoAR-
IsAJe_lcq8z_E09GzfidvRF40VdSpU1lXz9yjDOOFoPGkduzxz_GfNj6-NY-
qIaAuLhEALw_wcB
Ismail, A., Mahmud, A., Nimalini, A., and Ajeng, T. (2009) Health Tourism
in Malaysia: The Strengths and Weaknesses. *Journal of Community Health*,
15(1), 7–15.
Kuala Lumpur Health and Medical Hospitals (2018) Top Ten Hospitals in Kuala
Lumpur. https://en.yelp.my/search?cflt=hospitals&find_loc=Kuala+Lumpur
Land Public Transport Commission Malaysia (2018) About SPAD. www.
spad.gov.my/about-spad/overview
Lehmann, S. (2010) *The Principles of Green Urbanism: Transforming the City
for Sustainability*. Washington, DC: Earthscan.
Lim, Z. H. (2017) Kopitiam Ekonomi and the Construction of the Malaysia Ne-
oliberal Subject. In: S. G. Yeoh, ed. *Malaysians and Their Identities*. Petaling
Jaya: Strategic Information and Research Development Centre, pp. 63–85.
Limkokwing University (2018) www.limkokwing.net/malaysia/about/campus
Llewelyn-Davies (2000) Urban Design Compendium English Partnerships
and Housing Corporation.
Malaysia Department of Statistics (2018) Social Statistics Bulletin Malaysia.
https://dosm.gov.my/v1/index.php?r=column/cthemeByCat&cat=152&bul_
id=NU5hZTRkOSs0RVZwRytTRE5zSitLUT09&menu_id=U3VPM-
ldoYUxzVzFaYmNkWXZteGduZz09
Malaysian Roads (2018) General Information. www.piarc.org/ressources/
documents/1216,road-network-in-malaysia-v2.pdf
Morshidi, S., and Abdul Rahim, A. (2010) Going Global: Development, Risks
and Responses in Kuala Lumpur and Putrajaya. In: S. Hamnet and D.
Forbes, eds. *Planning Asian Cities: Risks and Resilience*. London and New
York: Routledge, pp. 220–240
New Straight Times (2018) Boosting the Reading Habit, February 2019. www.
nst.com.my/education/2018/07/394232/boosting-reading-habit
NZSIF (2018) What Is Social Infrastructure. www.nzsif.co.nz/Social-
Infrastructure/What-is-Social-Infrastructure/
Pigeon, M. (2012) Soggy Politics: Making Water Public in Malaysia. In: M.
Pigeon, D. McDonald, O. Hoedeman, and S. Kishimoto, eds. *Remunicipal-
isation: Putting Water Back into Public Hands*. Amsterdam: Transnational
Institute, pp. 90–106.
PR1MA (2018) About PR1MA. www.pr1ma.my/about.php?lang=en
Publishing Perspectives (2018) https://publishingperspectives.com/2015/07/
germany-a-nation-of-readers/
Purcell, M. (2011) Neoliberalisation and Democracy. In: S. Fainstein and S.
Campbell, eds. *Readings in Urban Theory*. London: John Wiley and Sons,
pp. 42–55.
Qeuk, D. (2014) The Malaysian Health Care System: A Review. www.re-
searchgate.net/publication/237409933_The_Malaysian_Health_Care_
System_A_Review

Skyscanner (2018) Kuala Lumpur International Airport. www.skyscanner. com.my/airports/kul/kuala-lumpur-international-airport.html?ksh_ id=_k_CjwKCAiAiJPkBRAuEiwAEDXZZY-y3MO7K0tB7Qw2yHu UHP4nRrE65hJ0OfMurOM9fb674psYXnwe2RoC7wYQAvD_ BwE_k_&associateID=SEM_GGF_00065_00025&utm_source=google& utm_medium=cpc&utm_campaign=MY-Flights-Search-EN-DSA-RL-SA&utm_term=&kpid=google_1495801363_60503784671_285818933736_ aud-326758276298:dsa-485627260518_c_&gcl id=CjwKCAiAiJPkBRAuEiw AEDXZZY-y3MO7K0tB7Qw2yHuUHP4nRrE65hJ0OfMurOM9f-b674psYXnwe2RoC7wYQAvD_BwE

Suruhanjaya Tenaga (Energy Commission Malaysia 2018) Overview of Energy Commission. www.st.gov.my/details/aboutus/1

SPAD (2016) Land Public Transport Transformation in Malaysia – History, Aspirations and Challenges. www.spad.gov.my/sites/default/ files/chairman_speech-22april2016l.pdf

SPAD (2018a) Commercial District Travel for Kuala Lumpur's Commuters. www.spad.gov.my/land-public-transport/rail/commercial-district-travel-kuala-lumpurs-commuters

SPAD (2018b) Klang Valley Mass Rapid Transit (KVMRT) Project. www. spad.gov.my/land-public-transport/rail/klang-valley-mass-rapid-transit-kvmrt-project

SPAD (2018c) KTM Commuter: Convenient Intercity Travel for Everyday Journeys and Seasonal Trips. www.spad.gov.my/land-public-transport/ rail/convenient-intercity-travel-everyday-journeys-and-seasonal-trips

SPAD (2018d) Reliable and Accessible Travel to the Airports. www.spad.gov. my/land-public-transport/rail/reliable-and-accessible-travel-airports

Study Malaysia (2018) List of Universities in Malaysia. https://afterschool.my/ private-colleges-in-kuala-lumpur

Study in London (2019) Universities in London. www.studylondon.ac.uk/ universities

Study in the UK (2019) Private Universities in the UK. www.studying-in-uk. org/private-universities-in-uk/

Subang International Airport (2018) www.kuala-lumpur.ws/airport/subang-international-airport.htm

Suruhanjaya Tenaga (Energy Commission Malaysia) (2017) Energy Malaysia 2. www.st.gov.my/ms/contents/publications/energyMalaysia/EM12%20 Nov%202017%20v2.pdf

Tee, Go, A., Tee, A., and Yahaya (2011) Public Low-Cost Housing in Malaysia: Case Studies on PPR Low-Cost Flats in Kuala Lumpur. www.researchgate. net/publication/266502429_Public_Low-Cost_Housing_in_Malaysia_ Case_Studies_on_PPR_Low-Cost_Flats_in_Kuala_Lumpur

Telekom Malaysia (2018) Corporate Malaysia. www.tm.com.my/corporate/ Pages/corporate_profile.html

Tenaga National Berhad (2018) Company History. www.tnb.com.my/ about-tnb/history/

The Star Online (2019) Malaysia Ranks 1st in the World's Best Healthcare Category. www.thestar.com.my/news/nation/2019/02/07/malaysia-ranks-1st-in-worlds-best-healthcare-category/

Transcore (2017) Kuala Lumpur. www.railway-technology.com/projects/kuala-lumpur-driverless-metro/

Trip Advisor Kuala Lumpur (2018) Concerts and Shows in Kuala Lumpur. www.tripadvisor.com.my/Attractions-g298570-Activities-c58-Kuala_Lumpur_Wilayah_Persekutuan.html

UNESCO (2016) Culture Urban Future. Global Report on Culture for Sustainable Urban Development. Manual. UNESCO, Paris, France.

University of Malaya (2018) Telecommunications in Malaysia. http://studentsrepo.um.edu.my/1311/2/CHAP_1.pdf

Xianmin University (2019) Facts of Xianmin University, Malaysia. www.xmu.edu.my/2017/0525/c14682a320796/page.htm

Zainon, N., Mohd Rahim, A. F., Sulaiman, S., Abd Karim, S. B., and Hamzah, A. (2017) Factors Affecting the Demand of Affordable Housing among the Middle Income Groups in Klang Valley Malaysia. *Journal of Design and Built Environment*, Special Issue December 2017, 1–10.

6 Spatial practices—dividing and connecting

Introduction

This chapter analyses further examples of socio-spatial infrastructure in KL used by citizens from different religious, ethnic and economic backgrounds. Similarities and differences between how (and when) members of different communities are using the same spaces are explored. The role of material infrastructure as a mediator between different communities is examined. This expands the ANT-inspired methodology, making also references to New Materialism as a useful conceptual framework.

Material objects and spaces have agency. This is a fundamental assumption when talking about the built environment in KL. Space itself could be understood as a relationship, but it could also be seen as 'being'. This dual existence, "...space is simultaneously relational and ontological" (Nieuwenhuis, 2014) allows us to discuss not only practices happening in space but also to see space as an active being/object. But what does it mean that objects have an agency?

Materiality of agency

Just to give an example of the agency of an object, we can imagine the agency of an electronic keycard to a hotel room, in contrast to the agency of a traditional key with a big room number tag (Latour, 1991). One can quickly put the keycard into their wallet, the conventional key with a big, hefty tag needs to be put into the bag, or a pocket, but it may be pretty uncomfortable. It means that the keycard and traditional key influence the way that the hotel guest may dress and then how s/he behaves. It is not very difficult to imagine the different scenarios triggered by different outfits. Different clothes, different shoes shape the way how we move, how we behave, what we can and cannot do.

The built environment does the same but on a much larger scale. The surface of a pavement influences the way how people walk, for whom the walking could be easier or more difficult. The location of a street crossing may affect the movement patterns of a vast number of people. The location of shade, the existence of canopies, benches and every element of the built environment one can imagine influences and shapes the social life of a city. The materials used for pavements influence how people walk, or even how different people (because of wearing different types of shoes) walk differently. One does not see materials as passive, but rather (clearly influenced by New Materialism) the matter as active and entangled with any human activities. The interaction we are interested in happens between human beings, their clothes and other artificial equipment they use (for example, glasses) and elements of the built environment. Only by looking at this kind of plexus, it is possible to understand what the city does to its residents and why.

Sometimes, the materiality seems a secondary factor. When analysing the most successful shopping centres in KL, we should probably take into account the diversity of the program, the number of attractions available for customers. But these attractions are also spatially distributed, and they are constructed (like, for example, the ice ring in Sunway Pyramid). One of the most important factors making shopping centres so popular in KL is their air-conditioned space, with accessible (mostly free) toilets and a significant number of restaurants and bars. As it is mentioned in previous chapters, shopping centres are incredibly successful in breaking ethnic and religious boundaries (however, obviously, they create other divisions based on economic status). The layout of shopping centres ignores religious divisions—food court puts together restaurants serving and not serving halal food. Shopping centres are closer to the old Soviet model of the social condenser (Murawski, 2017; Rendell, 2017) than to the public space - they force customers to be close to each other, to see each other and to recognise each other. They can't force people to interact, but these spaces could put users in a situation where interactions may happen. It may be painful to admit, but shopping centres seem to be one of the most successful instruments leading to social inclusion and cross-ethnic and cross-religious interactions in KL.

To understand the meaning of the built environment as a mechanism of inclusion better, this study goes beyond an ontology focused on singular being/subject (singular existence) and engage with an ontology of coexistence. New Materialism promises to go beyond dualistic worldview, and this is also the approach we are happy to take. From this perspective, it is not the actor (or as it's called in ANT—actant) that matters, but 'the act' itself. It is important to focus on the mechanism of interaction between subjects, not on the subjects themselves. Therefore, when discussing the presence of any actor in the city, it is imperative to focus on the relationship between this particular actor and other actors. The relationship is essential, not actors themselves. The relationship defines actors, and this acting plexus becomes a new entity we should analyse. Below is an example of food consumption in Kuala Lumpur.

> A plethora of hawker stalls is a multicultural minefield. Malays do not eat at Chinese stalls where pork may have been prepared, Indians seek out Indian stalls where no beef is on offer or only vegetarian fare is prepared.
>
> (Sardar, 2000, p. 95)

However, when one thinks about a Chinese restaurant that serves pork, one should see this restaurant as a node of a broad network of actors and spaces that excludes Muslim customers, companies and workers. The restaurant itself will be probably a space where Muslim customers of the city can't be seen—but what about the supply chain? What about all of these spaces where pork is produced, prepared, stored and transported? For practising Muslims, all these spaces are haram, if we think about explicit spatial exclusion—these spaces are an excellent example of how and where it happens.

> ...the Quran, clearly states that pork and liquor are forbidden from the Islamic point of view (...) However, if there is contamination between Halal and Haram, the Halal is contaminated and become non-Halal. Therefore, a Halal supply chain should, first of all, guarantee that there is no contamination between Halal and Haram. As also argued by all persons interviewed, the Halal product matters at the point of consumption. Therefore, the whole supply chain needs to be addressed to protect the integrity of a Halal product.
>
> (Tieman, 2011)

Any business involved in Islamic economy (what is especially important when considering financial aspects of economics) is automatically excluded from any activities related to pork-production:

> One of the major innovations in the financial community is the rapid growth of Islamic financial services around the world.

Today, Sharia-compliant assets amount to $939 billion worldwide. (...)... companies whose core business involves alcohol, conventional financial services, entertainment, pork-related products, tobacco, or weapons are excluded.

(Walkshäusl and Lobe, 2012)

There are spaces devoted to produce and distribute pork, which will be separated from places where Muslims in KL could be found, but the very act of selling pork-based dishes influences space far beyond just an area occupied by seller and buyer (consumer). The smell of a particular food could be seen as attempts to claim a more significant part of the city public space:

Bakkuah is a sweetly-seasoned pork mince, which is flattened into sheets and barbequed over a charcoal fire until it is a glistening deep red, smoky and lightly charred. It is a favoured gift during the Chinese New Year period (...). There's this street in KL [Kuala Lumpur], Petaling Street, which is in the old China Town and every Chinese New Year; it's full of shops selling bakkuah, and they cover the whole street with smoke. Now that's something that I always remember growing up with, especially around Chinese New Year, when you could hardly walk through the street without coughing a bit, just because the smoke was so thick. But that time when I went back [in the mid-1990s], my dad was telling me how there was a bit of trouble... this was the way he put it, there were a few complaints from more devout Muslims members of the community because they couldn't actually walk down the street at all.

(Choo, 2011)

Choo (2011) also stresses that three main different religious groups in KL live according to slightly different calendars—defined by religious festivals. The combination of time, space, legal regulations and less tangible (but still spatial and material) elements like soundscapes and smellscapes illustrate the difficulty to find common ground across religious and ethnic groups in Malaysian society. Similar mechanisms will work concerning beef as excluding Hindu believers living in the city. Pork and beef have an agency. These products drastically change the way that the city—its spaces and institutions—functions. The agency of objects and spaces could work to exclude particular users or to build connections and platforms, allowing and supporting interactions. Less strictly, one can observe a specific group of Muslim, avoiding places where alcohol is served. In another example related to religions, we have found traders selling flowers in front of a Hindu temple with buyers coming from diverse communities, and they buy flowers not only for religious purposes. We have seen halal restaurants in which not only Muslims eat. Religion can have exclusive power, but it could also have inclusive elements and mechanisms. The significant number of charities operating in KL is at least inspired by the particular ethical system, rooted in a specific religion.

It could be assumed that public spaces in the city are the spaces that unify the diverse social activities or at least these spaces can support social interactions between members of different social, ethnic and religious groups. However, it should be said that in our opinion, public spaces in KL are not working as spaces of encounters and random interaction. As it was argued previously, we have doubts whether the very idea of 'public space,' as such, is relevant in this particular South Asian city. Obviously, people do interact across ethnic and religious divisions, but these interactions are established in places of work or study, not in open, urban spaces. In the research done more than 20 years ago on interethnic interactions, Nobaya Ahmad found that about 30% of Malays and Chinese (research was focused on these two ethnic groups) are reluctant to have a neighbour from another ethnic group (Ahmad, 2000). There is no reason to believe this percentage drastically changed.

One can observe multi-ethnic and multi-religious groups on the street or in the restaurant, but one can't see how these groups are formed in these spaces. This is a reason that analysing the inclusive and exclusive forces working through the built environment is so important. There are at least three reasons why it is essential to question the intellectual value of the public space as a conceptual framework to analyse urban areas in KL and social interactions one can observe in non-private urban spaces. One reason is the climate, the other is a car-oriented urban structure, and the third is Islam. The KL is a tropical city, where temperature oscillates around 30 degree Celsius and humidity around 80%. There are no months without rain, the driest month is July (around 50 mm) and the rainiest in November (about 200 mm). The weather like this is not the best for walking and for spending time in open space. Kuala Lumpur has many green spaces, but very few of them could be called urban parks. KLCC Park is a special case (Kozlowski et al., 2015; Ayeghi and Ujang, 2017), surrounded by hotels and offices, attached to one of the most successful shopping centres in the city; therefore, it is probably the most successful park in KL. The success of this particular place seems related to the car-oriented structure and the lifestyle dominant in the city—KLCC has a massive car park; however, it has also connections to the rest of the city via public transport, especially KL Light Rail Transit (LRT). But even this park is not very popular, especially during the day. The peak of its popularity may be seen at late afternoons and evenings. It is related clearly to drop of temperature, but also to some visual attractions in the park, which may be seen after dark. This plexus of a place with purposes (proximity to shopping centre plus visual attractions) and the particular conditions—pleasant temperature and relative darkness—allow people to gather and interact. KLCC Park (after dark) is a good example how the mechanism of stimulated inclusivity could work—there must be spatial and not spatial conditions to allow people to be together, to be brave enough to question ethnic and religious boundaries.

Figure 6.1 shows cafes and shopping malls in Kuala Lumpur and surrounding areas catering for different ethnic groups. It is clearly visible that although they share one space, they do not interact with

(a)   (b)

(c)   (d)

Figure 6.1 Cafes and shopping malls in the KLMR catering for all ethnic groups. Although ethnic groups share the same space, they very seldom socially interact with each other.

Source: M. Kozlowski.

each other. This phenomenon is typical for public and private realm spaces in the KLMR and in most parts of Malaysia.

The agency of spaces and objects is the point of departure, but the issue investigated here is slightly more controversial. A focus on the ontology of coexistence means that the thinking in this study is non-dialectical. In discussing mechanisms of inclusion and exclusion, we do not focus on contradictions and conflicts, but on ways that diverse forces and actors interact. To some extent, this perspective is related to the idea of intersectionality. Returning to the example discussed above, the restaurant as a particular space could be exclusive because of access issues. The restaurant as an organisation could have specific rules on whether or not to allow the general public to enter. Specific menus can exclude believers of certain religions. The spatial aspect is important, but it is not the only aspect to consider. The relationship between spatial and non-spatial forces (religious beliefs, cultural habits, lifestyle choices) is not dialectical, the non-spatial forces actualise in space. However, space itself is hierarchical and has its own agency. As Nawratek (2018) has previously discussed:

> ...to get from point A to point B, we need to overcome the space between (let's call it X) and our willingness to reach the point B, which gives space X its importance, putting it in a position of strength that can decide whether or not to allow us to get to the point B. This immanent hierarchy of space must, however, always be placed in a wider spatial context (we can bypass space X, we can find alternative paths) and in a context that is not spatial, although it actualises itself in space (we can establish the law to 'force' space X not to restrict access from space A to space B). This non-spatial context is founded on a narrative (a story or a law) which prompts us to move from point/space A to point/space B (in the chapter we referred to above, we make a distinction between space and a point). This narrative gives importance and meaning to space B.
>
> (Nawratek, 2018)

The discussion on space is related closely to the idea of 'spatial justice' as discussed by Edward Soja, David Harvey and others. Accessibility to particular parts of urban infrastructure by specific groups of residents (or individual residents) is crucial when discussing the inclusivity of urban spaces.

Main findings

Ben Hillier's configurational theory of space makes clear that spatial relationships are hierarchical. It means it is essential to discuss power relationships when analysing the inclusive/exclusive aspects of urban spaces. Access, the ability to go through particular space, gives this space power of control. Who controls access, controls the movement in the city. Described above mechanism of spatial segregation is not based solely on the spatial distribution of accessible elements of urban infrastructure—this mechanism is instead a combination of material, spatial and cultural landscapes and narratives, where and when exclusion and inclusion are constructed in a particular moment and place. This is probably the most critical observation to focus on—these mechanisms are not fixed, not defined once and forever. Inclusion could be achieved when it is carefully designed—it is never permanent and can't be universalised. Still it could be continuously constructed over and over again.

Bibliography

Ahmad, N. (2000) The Social and Spatial Impact of Settlement Policies in Kuala Lumpur, Malaysia. Doctoral dissertation, University of Sheffield.

Ayeghi, A., and Ujang, N. (2017) The Impact of Physical Features on User Attachment to Kuala Lumpur City Centre (KLCC) Park, Malaysia. *Geografia-Malaysian Journal of Society and Space*, 10(3), 32.

Choo, S. (2011) Meeting in the Market: The Constitution of Seasonal, Ritual, and Inter-Cultural Time in Malaysia. *Continuum*, 25(5), 619–635, DOI:10.1080/10304312.2011.597844

Kozlowski, M., Ujang, N., and Maulan, S. (2015) Performance of Public Spaces in the Kuala Lumpur Metropolitan Region in Terms of the Tropical Climate. *AlamCipta*, 8(1), 41–51.

Latour, B. (1991) Technology Is Society Made Durable. In J. Law, ed. *A Sociology of Monsters: Essays on Power, Technology and Domination*. London: Routledge, pp. 103–131.

Murawski, M. (2017) Introduction: Crystallising the Social Condenser. *The Journal of Architecture*, 22(3), 372–386, DOI:10.1080/13602365.2017.1322815

Nawratek, K. (2018) Architecture of Radicalized Postsecularism. In J. Beaumont, ed. *The Routledge Handbook of Postsecularity*. London: Routledge, pp. 315–324.

Nieuwenhuis, M. (2014) Taking Up the Challenge of Space: New Conceptualisations of Space in the Work of Peter Sloterdijk and Graham Harman. *Continent*, 4(1), 16–37.

Rendell, J. (2017) Conclusion: The Social Condenser—A Thing in Itself? *The Journal of Architecture*, 22(3), 578–583, DOI:10.1080/13602365.2017.1323996

Sardar, Z. (2000) *The Consumption of Kuala Lumpur.* London: Reaktion Books.

Tieman, M. (2011) The Application of Halal in Supply Chain Management: In-Depth Interviews. *Journal of Islamic Marketing,* 2(2), 186–195, DOI:10.1108/17590831111139893

Walkshäusl, C., and Lobe, S. (2012) Islamic Investing. *Review of Financial Economics,* 21(2), 53–62.

Concluding notes

In a world disintegrating in seemingly intractable divisions, conflicts and self-righteously justified hatreds, authors believe the topics covered in this book are immensely important. Kuala Lumpur urban spaces are relatively less scholarly addressed than their equivalent in other Southeast Asian cities; however, Kuala Lumpur and its metropolitan region are extremely interesting because of its demographic and spatial diversity. Malaysian political culture is similarly ingrained in the issues firmly rooted in ethnic and religious diversity of the country. Ethnicity continues to be a vital factor politically and socially; religions, as the book discussed, have severe economic consequences.

It is important to remember that in the recent history of Malaysia, the British and Dutch colonial administration systems had entered into agreements as well as the embeddedness of Malaysian Islam. The robust theoretical framework in this book gives the reader an intellectual tools to investigate KLMR's built environment, its legal, religious and political systems as well as the dominant cultural imagination. The book suggests to (re)read KLMR as the stage of constant dialogue and renegotiation. It also introduces a theoretical perspective focused on the socio-material dialectic of segregation/interaction between different communities in the metropolitan region. Following this perspective, every built element of KLMR should be seen as the particular stage for the creation of the 'communities of a higher-order' through the interaction with urban materiality. The book acknowledges a high level of fragmentation of KLMR, but at the same moment discusses possibilities and existing practices of inclusivity beyond just political slogans and educational campaigns.

The book argues that elements of urban infrastructure could work as an essential mediator 'beyond community', allowing inclusive urban social structures to be built, despite different cultural and religious tensions. Based on empirical study, it explores how different communities use the same spaces and shared elements of infrastructure in KL according to a theoretical framework accounting for both western and Islamic conceptualisations of the idea of community.

This book is framed by relational methodological perspectives (STS/ANT), which are very strongly focused on the materiality of the researched subject (built environment and its users). The theoretical framework gives readers intellectual tools to connect investigations of three different phenomena—built environment, legal system and cultural imagination—but a new theoretical conceptualisation is also an essential outcome of the book, contributing to the broader discussion on urban infrastructure and the multi-cultural, not western city. The book attempts to question conventional Western urban narratives and open paths to decolonise urban theoretical engagement.

By locating the subject of this book outside Europe, in a globalised, post-colonial and predominantly Muslim city, the book aims to contribute to the decolonised reflection on public spaces and urban infrastructure. Understanding the mechanisms of social cohesion is of urgent importance not only for policymakers, but also for urban designers, urban planners and other practitioners working in the built environment. Though limited to one city, this book aims to contribute towards the creation of more inclusive places in other multi-ethnic, multi-cultural and multi-religious communities. As well, the content of the book should provide an essential basis for planners and designers to design urban places in the city based on an understanding of the socio-political dimension of the KLMR, its urbanisation process and the historical perspectives of the people and places.

The book demonstrates that KLMR is undergoing a massive property-led redevelopment and rapidly transforming from an inclusive city to a global urban environment characterised by social polarisation and increased number of utopian private exclusive communities. However, there is a strong inclination among the urban community, especially the ethnic Malays, to retain local traditions by attaining public spaces for events such as religious festivities, weddings, social gatherings, and for activities, including outdoor eating and open food markets. It is a challenge for all local authorities in the metropolitan region to ensure that this good practice of everyday urbanism is continued in the future.

The content of the book oscillates between highly theoretical reflection on elements of Western, Islamic and Chinese urban and political theory and discussions on particular case studies and research done in KLMR. The ambition of the book is to provide limited (the format of the book series is relatively compact) but comprehensive description of the city and suggest a diverse set of narratives how the city could be read and interpreted. The book is not providing any ultimate conclusions; it is not a manual on how to create an inclusive KLMR. However, authors believe that it gives a set of tools to understand better and to engage more in-depth into the process of making KLMR a better place. Authors believe KL gives a unique opportunity to intellectually test new urban narratives, to speculate about diverse, inclusive city rooted in non-Western (or not-only-Western) traditions. Kuala Lumpur and its surrounding urban conurbation is not that city (yet), as authors discussed in the book—the current form of the city seems less inclusive than it was at the beginning of independent Malaysia. Despite this, authors believe that the new form of inclusivity is slowly emerging in the city, and the book gives intellectual tools to help understand how this (radical) inclusivity could be achieved.

Index

Note: *Italic* page numbers refer to figures and page numbers followed by "n" denote endnotes.

Printed in the United States
by Baker & Taylor Publisher Services